"Personal achievement advice has been with us since time immemorial, but in *The Way of the Warrior Saint*, an American parish priest from Arizona, Fr. Chris Salamy, takes it to another level by overlaying a powerfully Christian teaching on top of the traditional wisdom of the ages. His unique message for exceptional living, through what he terms a crucifixional life, is an important concept and a must read, especially for all dads and younger men."

—Dean G. Popps, former Assistant Secretary of the United States Army

"*The Way of the Warrior Saint* is a helpful read for anyone who is trying to put faith into action. It is filled with real life challenges, engaging stories, solid principles, and practical tips to help the reader navigate life's uncertainties with clear direction. Father Chris distills his years of ministry experience into memorable and applicable 'takeaways' that can help each one of us and all of us live a life that honors God and serves others."

—Tim Tassopoulos, President and COO, Chick-fil-A, Inc.

"In *The Way of the Warrior Saint*, Fr. Chris draws from his personal experiences to paint a vivid and compelling case for taking up the 'crucifixional' way of life. Not only does Fr. Chris inspire his reader but he also gently guides them towards a fuller Christian life. I highly recommend this often humorous and bare-knuckled book by one of the Church's preeminent pastors it will engage every reader who wants to live courageously for Christ."

—Father Evan Armatas, Host of *Orthodoxy Live* on Ancient Faith Radio and author of *Toolkit for Spiritual Growth: A Practical Guide to Prayer, Fasting, and Almsgiving*

"In this inspirational work, Fr. Chris explores the three fundamental relationships of man – himself, others, and work – through the lens of Crucifixional Living. Providing practical steps along the way, the reader is challenged with each chapter to enact these steps in their lives to unlock the greatness that lies within. Fr. Chris proves himself a maverick amidst a sea of mindlessness, providing a voice of reason during what continue to be challenging times."

—Gregory J. Abdalah, D.Min., Pastoral Assistant, St. George Antiochian Orthodox Church Phoenix, AZ, Assistant Professor of Pastoral Theology, St. Vladimir's Orthodox Theological Seminary

"*The Way of the Warrior Saint* is a work of art. Fr. Chris identifies the missing link in our lives that allows us to conquer anything and live successfully. The concept of living a crucifixional life to overcome and win is genius and a tool that everyone should embody. This book is a must read for anyone that has faced challenges and wants to live more powerfully."

—Dr. Eric J. Scroggins, author of Vision Blockers, life
& business coach, CEO of EricScroggins.com

"Fr. Chris Salamy's new book *The Way of the Warrior Saint* is a spiritually uplifting yet real world-based prescription for how to find success on the playing field or floor, in everyday life, and in your spiritual pursuit; all of which have more similarities than many people generally recognize.

"Each chapter explores a specific topic related to finding greater success in how we can lead our lives and puts that topic into a greater context. The book then incorporates certain scriptural passages and closes with Practical Points that help make the prescriptions easier to incorporate into your everyday life.

"Having built championship teams, I find many of the principles of success in this book remarkably familiar. Living a Crucifixional Life is difficult. The path to any ultimate victory in sports or life or a spiritual pursuit always comes through a sort of death and rebirth experience. Once you have gone through this process you will always recognize it in numerous other parts of your life.

"Self-sacrifice becomes the necessity to reach the worthiest goals. Not until Superstars sacrifice their selfish goals to make their teammates better can they reach the mountaintop of a championship and the sort of immortality that championship provides. Failure to learn this lesson, in life or sports, condemns one to a life of mediocrity.

"As Father Chris makes clear, this type of sacrifice and hard work is not the easy path. Growth and learning are inherently uncomfortable. True transformational change and success only takes place at the edge of our comfortable experience, (and I would argue just past it).

"*The Way of the Warrior Saint* can help you make the path to something as grand as enlightenment, or as simple as being a better family member a success. Pick it up and 'Go Get Some.'"

—Steve Patterson, President of Pro Sports Consulting

"To be a Christian, Paul tells us, is to be a warrior or an athlete. Addressed to young adults, Fr Chris Salamy opens up, in a very immediate way, what it means to live a crucifixional life. Filled with practical insights and lessons, this book is both challenging and encouraging. 'Go get some!'

—Fr. John Behr, Regius Chair of Humanity, University of
Aberdeen and Metropolitan Kallistos Chair of Orthodox
Theology, Vrije Universiteit, Amsterdam

"Wisdom is more precious than fine gold. In an era largely accepting of situational integrity, self-help ideology and the empty pain it creates, Fr. Chris clearly illuminates the path to inner greatness and a joyful life found only in sacrificial living. Quit being simple minded and "get some."

—Mike Thayer, President and Senior Wealth Management
Advisor, Private Asset Management, Inc.

THE WAY OF THE WARRIOR SAINT

How to Live a Crucifixional Life

FR. CHRISTOPHER SALAMY

WESTBOW
PRESS®
A DIVISION OF THOMAS NELSON
& ZONDERVAN

This book is a work of non-fiction. Unless otherwise noted, the author and the publisher make no explicit guarantees as to the accuracy of the information contained in this book and in some cases, names of people and places have been altered to protect their privacy.

WestBow Press books may be ordered through booksellers or by contacting:

WestBow Press
A Division of Thomas Nelson & Zondervan
1663 Liberty Drive
Bloomington, IN 47403
www.westbowpress.com
844-714-3454

Because of the dynamic nature of the Internet, any web addresses or links contained in this book may have changed since publication and may no longer be valid. The views expressed in this work are solely those of the author and do not necessarily reflect the views of the publisher, and the publisher hereby disclaims any responsibility for them.

Any people depicted in stock imagery provided by Getty Images are models, and such images are being used for illustrative purposes only.
Certain stock imagery © Getty Images.

Interior Image Credit: Fr. Chris Salamy

[Scripture quotations are] from the Revised Standard Version of the Bible, copyright © 1946, 1952, and 1971 the Division of Christian Education of the National Council of the Churches of Christ in the United States of America. Used by permission. All rights reserved.

Scripture quotations taken from The Holy Bible, New International Version® NIV® Copyright © 1973 1978 1984 2011 by Biblica, Inc. TM. Used by permission. All rights reserved worldwide.

ISBN: 978-1-6642-1945-8 (sc)
ISBN: 978-1-6642-1944-1 (hc)
ISBN: 978-1-6642-1946-5 (e)

Library of Congress Control Number: 2021901541

Print information available on the last page.

WestBow Press rev. date: 01/28/2021

CONTENTS

For my best girl.
Without whom I would be lost.

INTRODUCTION

"I can't feel the left side of my face."

Saying those words to myself at 3:47 a.m. on a Sunday morning was a little bit disconcerting. I awoke with a pounding headache, the likes of which I've never experienced. I've never had a migraine, but if this was what it was like, then I never wanted to have another one again. It was brutal.

I had to be at my church by 8:00 a.m. to prepare for that day's services, and I was hopeful I could go back to sleep for a couple of hours beforehand. My headache grew worse, and rather than disturb my bride with more tossing and turning, I got out of bed to wander around the house for a bit. My wandering led me to open my laptop in the family room. Perhaps *ESPN.com* would have some early headlines before the NFL games kicked off for the day. But then something really strange happened. I noticed that I couldn't see the left side of the screen. I could see the headlines section on the right side of the screen, but the entire left side of the screen was blurry. As the headache intensified, I realized that something wasn't right. I'm a pretty healthy guy and take my physical well-being seriously so this was particularly scary. I tried rubbing my left eye hoping to bring some focus to the screen, yet when I did, I realized I couldn't feel it. My face, I mean. I couldn't feel my face. This was strange because I knew my face was there. I'd always had a left side of my face so it had to be there. But still, I couldn't feel myself rubbing the left side of my face. At this point I knew something was totally wrong. So, I did what every super macho dude would do and went back to bed. I'd just "rub some dirt on it", sleep it off and when I'd wake up everything would be better. Except it wasn't. The headache got worse and the left side of my face went totally numb. Finally, I decided I had to act and drove myself to the emergency room.

It turns out I was experiencing a transient ischemic attack (TIA). More commonly known as a mini-stroke, a TIA happens when the blood supply to a part of the brain is blocked for a short period of time. Thankfully less damaging than an actual stroke, a TIA was nonetheless a wake-up call. It was a sign that God was giving me a second chance and I'd better not blow it. Things in my life absolutely had to change. And they had to change immediately. As a husband, a father of two young daughters and the pastor of a large and growing church community, I still had a lot to do, and I was determined to accomplish everything God had assigned me.

Something radical was needed to do this and couldn't be a temporary change. I needed something permanent and serious. But I didn't know exactly what to do. I didn't know exactly where to look or who to ask to find my answer. Always a voracious reader, I turned toward to my most trusted source of learning: books. I read little books, big books, audio books, scientific books, theology books, psychology books, efficiency books, self-help books, funny books, boring books, classic books and e-books. I read absolutely everything I could get my hands on. It was the most intense period of study in my life, more so, even, than when I was earning my doctorate. I was determined to find that one easy fix that would change my life for the better. There absolutely had to be a magic pill that would help me effect a positive and lasting change in my life, and when I found it, I was going to swallow it. I had had a TIA and I wasn't going back.

To my surprise, all of the reading and all of the study left me feeling a little underwhelmed. I had accomplished a lot, to be sure, and some of the material was indeed impressive. And though I would implement a lot of what I learned into my life, the hole still felt empty. I needed something more. I knew there would be a click inside my gut when I found it.

The emptiness I was feeling was born out of a mindset I had submitted to and is the prevailing mindset of our world today: life should be easy. We shouldn't work harder, we just need to work smarter. We shouldn't have to wake up early to run five miles, we just need to take some magic fat-burning pill to get ripped abs. I don't have to sacrifice my desires to have a healthy relationship with my spouse. If it doesn't go my way, I'll just bail. Make sure that prenup is solid. It's like we're being told to find that one easy solution or program or formula that will lead you to success and all you have to do is follow it. If you find the right system with the right charts and the right acronyms, you will be free to focus on your passions so you can live a happier life. And isn't a happier life what everyone wants?

So, how's that happier life working out for everyone? The data seems to point to a lot less happiness in the world today. It appears that easy may not work after all. Let's be clear. I do think life should be simple. But simple is a far cry from easy. As my teacher used to ask his students, "Do you want to know the difference between simple and easy? Ask any mother how she gives birth to a baby."

I believe we default into easy because we're afraid. Yeah, that's right. I said it. Doing easy is borne from fear. The fear of discomfort. The fear of pain. The fear of failure. The fear of not being liked. The fear of losing ego. The fear of being wrong. Perhaps even the fear of admitting we have fear. Whatever particularly frightful thing we can imagine, it usually instigates our choice to take the easy road. As my TIA proved, I was knee-deep in doing things the easy way. And it landed me in the ER.

As ridiculous as it may sound, could hard actually be the way to go? Could it be that all of the quick fixes we've been sold over the years are nothing more than empty words? If we want to win at life, if we want to be truly successful in all the things we do, do we have to battle our monsters and fight and scrap and be afraid and grind and do the hard things? You bet we do. In the Epistle to the Ephesians, the Apostle Paul exhorts Christians to prepare for this battle, not necessarily with the world, but within ourselves. He asks us to, "[p]ut on the whole armor of God, that you may be able to stand against the wiles of the devil," (Revised Standard Version, Eph 6:11). He's asking us to be warriors and saints.

I'm a runner. Okay, not really. But I run for cardio. Okay, not really. I waddle. But each day I'm out there doing it, grinding and trying to stay healthy. One year, my church was sponsoring a 5K for a charitable organization we often work with. I'd never run in any kind of formal race and I wanted to post a respectable time, especially since I was probably going to be one of the oldest dudes in the race. I trained hard. Each day I hit the road to train, but for the life of me, I couldn't break thirty minutes for the 5K. Thirty minutes for 3.12 miles is not fast for most, but for me it was a great target and I was afraid I wasn't going to be able to hit it.

On the day of the race I was determined to finally break the thirty-minute mark. I started out smoothly and paced myself off of a true runner in front of me. The first mile was all right, but then it began to dawn on me that I was pacing myself off of a far better runner than myself and I was going to run out of gas. The next two miles were some of the hardest miles I've ever run. At no point was it fun. I wanted to slow down and take an easier pace at least ten times in the last mile alone. My legs were burning, my lungs were burning, my feet were burning. I thought I was going to throw up on two different occasions. It would have been so much easier to just slow down or even walk for a bit. Somehow, perhaps by God's grace, I didn't give in to the desire to take it easy. I waged war with a mind that begged me to take it easy. I simply said no. I dug as deep as I could and kept fighting. It was perhaps one of the hardest things I've ever done, if not the hardest. But I didn't slow down and I didn't quit.

In the grand scheme of things, running that last mile without quitting wasn't really an amazing feat. Many people do similar things all the time. But it taught me something powerful: easy would not help me break the thirty-minute barrier. Facing the hard things and conquering my monsters would. All of the suffering I went through in that last mile led me to finish in third place. And in 27:44. My fastest 5K time ever.

I learned an important lesson in that race: the way to conquer life's challenges comes from ignoring the easy road, confronting difficult things head on and living a sacrificial life. Victory comes from being a Warrior Saint. That's it. That's the only way success is won. We call that The Way of the Warrior Saint. The way to conquer your monsters is not easy. It's actually hard. Really hard. You will have to fight and grind and suffer and experience pain and weep and sweat and bleed. You're going to have to do things you don't want to do. But you know what? You actually want that. The world certainly tries to peddle lies of comfort and ease, but deep down inside, you crave that feeling of being alive when having confronted your monster face-to-face and won. Will you get bruised and beaten up? Sure. But you will be victorious. There is no other feeling that makes a person feel more alive than when he has conquered his monsters.

Think I'm making this up? Think again. Why do our most popular stories follow the same premise of facing off against monsters? Luke Skywalker had to fight Darth Vader. Harry Potter had Voldemort. Catniss had President Snow. Daenerys Stormborn had to face Cersei, and Jon Snow took on the Whitewalkers. Perseus had the Kraken. Horus had Set. Jesus had Sin and Death. Those stories all resonate with us because deep inside we know their stories are our stories. Their struggles are our struggles. Their fight is our fight. We can choose to ignore the fight with monsters, but that leads nowhere except into the abyss of mediocrity and insanity.

But if you want to unlock the greatness within you, I can show you a Way: The Way of the Warrior Saint. That's what this book is about: giving us practical and Biblically based wisdom on how to live a life that puts us on the way to greatness. Though our monsters are not necessarily mythological or magical beasts, they are nonetheless just as real in our lives. How do we fight with and conquer our monsters? The Warrior Saint does so by living a crucifixional life.

Let me explain what I mean by the word crucifixional. Taken from the Holy Bible, Jesus' story in all four of the Gospels ends in the same place. People assume that this means His Resurrection from the dead. Though that is certainly a crucial part of the message, that's not what I'm talking about. In fact, in the Gospel of Mark, the first gospel written historically, the original text ends at chapter 16 verse 8 with no appearance of Jesus after His Resurrection. (Verses 9-16 are later additions from an editor.) The text merely reveals that an angel told the women that He was raised from the dead. The climax of each of the Gospels is not the empty tomb. The climax of the story is on the Cross.

In Ancient Rome, one of the worst forms of torture, punishment and execution was crucifixion. Crucifixion was not designed to be quick. Criminals and political insurgents were often crucified as an example for others who would face a similar fate if they did not obey the mandates of the emperor. It was a painful and drawn out process and was not meant for those higher in society. For someone to have been crucified in Ancient Rome invariably meant that they were a loser of some sort. Heroes were not crucified.

The Gospel stories of Jesus take this mechanism and flip it upside down. Rather than being captured for lawlessness and revolution, the Gospels tell how Jesus voluntarily gave Himself up to death—death on a Cross, no less—in order to do something specific: to conquer Death itself. Oxymoronic as it may sound, that is the power of the story. Death is defeated by death. The Resurrection of Christ confirms that "it worked" by showing that the One who conquered the great monster Death by going through death was raised into a new life. His path to victory went from death into life, not the other way around.

Whether you are a Christian or not, the message of the Christ story is one that I believe is pertinent to all of humanity. You don't have to believe the tenets of the Christian faith to see that the mechanism of self-sacrifice is the way to find greatness within you. As noted above, even a cursory examination will reveal that the Christ story serves as the model for all of our great stories. Luke Skywalker had to throw away his light-saber and expose himself to the Emperor to truly become a Jedi at the end of the original Star Wars trilogy. Jon Snow had to sacrifice his beloved for the sake of the realm when he pierced Daenerys Stormborn. Harry Potter mirrors the Christ story when he dies and is resurrected at the end of the Deathly Hallows when the evil Voldemort is defeated.

But the crucifixional model isn't just for the movies. We can find the same message in sports. Kobe Bryant was a great example. He suffered and toiled in the early years of his career with the Lakers. Making the NBA playoffs for his first time, he lost to the Utah Jazz in the 1997 season. I'll never forget the airball he shot at the end of Game 5 and the look on his face after. He was so frustrated.

The very next year they advanced to the Conference Finals to play Utah again. This time the Lakers were swept by the Jazz. Guess what happened in 1999? They were swept again by the San Antonio Spurs. But Kobe was known as the hardest working player in the NBA. He never stopped working and never stopped grinding, and then something very different happened in the 2000 NBA Finals. Kobe and the Lakers won. The look on his face when he hoisted the trophy said it was all worth it. Kobe went on to win four more championships and is known as one of the greatest to ever play the game.

Another place which may seem strange to find crucifixional living is the kitchen. But it isn't really that strange if you think about it. Let's say you're on a diet and want to lose a few pounds, maintain good health and live a better life. I'd say you've set a noble goal. But you cannot succeed at that goal if you're going to eat Doritos and ice cream. It just doesn't work. And look, I'm not judging you. I picked Doritos and ice cream as examples because they're two of my biggest weaknesses. I've never eaten a Dorito . . . I either eat no Doritos or I eat all the Doritos. There is no in between for me. It's the same for ice cream. It is not hard to imagine me eating an entire pint of ice cream in one sitting. I love it. There have been countless times that my children have gone to the freezer to pull out a pint of Ben and Jerry's only to find it all eaten. And their mom just bought it yesterday.

But consuming either of those snacks is incompatible with my goal of living a healthy lifestyle and looking great at the beach. If I want to be healthy, I have to sacrifice my excessive desire to eat Doritos and ice cream. I can't have both. In some real sense, it is crucifixional because I am putting to death the desire to eat junk food in order to conquer the monster of poor health and flab. It's brutal to watch my kids eat my favorite treats, but it is so worth it when I drop a waist size.

These examples may seem trite at first glance, but I believe they are indicators of something much greater. Let them serve as metaphors for us to live a crucifixional life every day so that we can unleash the greatness that lies within us. You can have great health, a great marriage, great kids, great jobs, great careers, great spirituality, a great life. You can have that by joining the Way of the Warrior Saint and living a crucifixional life.

It's not fancy. It's gritty. There are no charts, graphs or fancy systems that will make you a better person if you follow all the steps in order. It is just the simple truth as revealed in Scripture. And you don't even have to be a Christian to recognize the truths revealed by the Gospel.

This book is not a religious tract per se, though it is saturated with Biblical wisdom. Rather, this is a book that teaches a life of the Cross—crucifixional living—as the only template for successful lives. In everything we do, we should copy how Jesus lived His life. Crucifixional living should become the *modus operandi* for success in your life. In each of the subsequent parts, we will explore mankind's relationship to three core elements of life. Part 1 explores mankind in relation to the self. It calls us to account in the battle versus pride and fear. Part 2 examines mankind in relation to others. Once we get ourselves right, we will focus on our interaction with others and how we can sacrifice for their sakes. Lastly, Part 3 offers guidance for mankind in relation to work. As this is the place where we spend the majority of our time, it necessitates thorough examination to better help us fight against inefficiency and excuses.

Each chapter will begin by examining a challenge we all struggle with in a relatable context. Next, we will hear God's input through a Biblical passage that will teach us how crucifixional living can conquer that particular challenge. Finally, each chapter will end with very simple and practical steps that can be implemented in your life immediately. Getting on the Way of the Warrior Saint simply requires that you start today. For what is teaching without action?

The following pages are filled with real life examples of people just like you and me who have found their greatness by living crucifixional lives. We will learn practical tools in order to battle against some of the monsters that each of us face in our daily lives. And we will hear Biblical wisdom and timeless truths that will inspire us to join the battle and stay strong in the face of the many challenges we face.

I don't believe that anything is impossible. I know you have it within you to find what you're looking for: that great life that you so desire to live. If you want that—and I know you do—then come along with me.

It's time to get some.

PART 1

MANKIND IN RELATION TO SELF

1

BEING COMFORTABLE BEING UNCOMFORTABLE

So much of what concerns our modern age is finding comfort. At the time of writing, the current trend in the fashion industry is loose fitting comfy clothing. We have a rough day at school or the office and look to eat comfort food. We hope to drive around in a comfortable car. We break up with a boyfriend or girlfriend via text message so it's not uncomfortable. Carvana helps you purchase your car without the discomfort of haggling with a pushy car salesman at the dealership. We have pills to help us lose weight, CBD oil to help us sleep, online purchasing so we don't have to talk to salespeople, Postmates so we can stay on the couch and Amazon to deliver just about anything.

I run between three and five miles each day. At least I try to. Well, I want to. But some mornings it's so much more comfortable under the warm covers than it is out on the road. It really isn't hard to convince myself that a few more minutes of sleep won't wreck the day's schedule. It's super easy to find an excuse—any excuse—to skip the run. I mean think about it. Under the blankets it's warm and soft and flat. It's so comfy. But out on the road it's hard. First of all, I don't really like running. It hurts. If you're doing it right, it hurts. Runners are supposed to push themselves to run harder and faster than they did the day before. Sometimes knees hurt or feet hurt or you can't breathe so well. Many mornings it's cold or raining or both. In the Sonoran Desert around Phoenix where I live, some mornings in the summer it reaches triple digit temperatures before 7:00 a.m. And besides, it's not as much fun as chilling in your bed playing on your cell phone watching YouTube videos or checking your Insta-feed!

§ BEING COMFORTABLE BEING UNCOMFORTABLE IN CONTEXT

It's taken many miles, but I've learned that comfort doesn't come without a cost. The guilt I feel because I was lazy and broke my run streak really bothers me throughout the day. I am a perfectionist and I love putting up long, perfect streaks. My Fitbit stars make me happy. Because of that, I have never regretted running. But I always regret not running. Staying comfortable also costs a new kind of streak: a streak of skipped runs. If you're like me, you can't easily rationalize getting back up and starting a new streak. Breaking a streak may seem like a small consequence for a little bit of comfort, but it is a sign of a much larger problem.

Skipping my runs has health consequences as well. I tend to eat better on days when I've done my cardio. I remind myself how hard the work was and ask, "Do you really want to throw all that hard work down the drain for some ice cream?" But if I skip my workout, it becomes super easy to justify any type of eating behavior. "Well, it's already been a bad day, I'll just start over tomorrow." I can't imagine I'm the only person to have had that internal conversation!

My mind is much clearer when I run, as well. It must be something about getting the blood pumping that really works wonders. It's amazing how much faster my brain works. My teaching metaphors are clearer and I draw mental lines faster. I notice a different level of quality in my teaching when I've started the day with a good sweat. Conversely, on days when I didn't get the juices flowing, I'm certainly not as sharp as I would like to be. My teaching might be good but it's not great. And I'm supposed to give great.

Human tendency is to default to the easy route. It's a lot more comfortable at the start. Long term, however, doing difficult and uncomfortable things is where the results really lie. Transformation, change, growth and success all happen at the edge of comfort. When you're in a place that is new and scary, you have the opportunity to take huge strides forward. Most people default to comfort. But I don't really want to be like most people. I'm fighting to live a crucifixional life so I can be exceptional. Remember, doing the easy things and staying comfortable is normal. And I don't want to be normal.

⸹ GOD'S INPUT

The story of Daniel shows what being comfortable being uncomfortable is like. In the first two chapters of the book, we learn that Daniel and his people were captives in Babylon. Because of their particular skills, Daniel and his three companions were directed to serve the king alongside the wise men of Babylon. One day, the king began having horrible dreams and was no longer able to sleep. Hoping to find solace and rest he called upon his wise men to interpret the dreams. Being terrified of the consequences if their interpretation did not please the king, none of the Babylonian wise men were willing to attempt it! In a fit of rage, the king decreed that all wise men should be put to death. Daniel entered the story at this point and asked for an audience with the king to interpret his dreams and hopefully save his life and the lives of his three friends. He blessed God in prayer the night before, took courage and presented himself to an angry, unrested king. At the conclusion of the story, Daniel gave an interpretation so satisfactory to the king of Babylon that he and his friends were rewarded with high ranking positions in the king's administration.

There are as many interpretations of this portion of Daniel as there are commentators, but it has always struck me how impressive Daniel was in this moment. Knowing that your head was about to be removed from your shoulders, would you ask for an audience with the wild man who issued the command to do it? What if your interpretation was wrong? Or worse, what if it was correct, but in his sleep-deprived craze, the king still wanted to chop your head off just for sport? Daniel knew that the environment he was entering literally meant life or death, but he didn't shy away from the moment. By being comfortable being uncomfortable, Daniel used what was a scary moment to take a huge stride forward.

After his encounter with the king, not only did he get to keep his head, but the king of Babylon, "gave Daniel high honors and many great gifts, and made him ruler over the whole province of Babylon, and chief prefect over all the wise men of Babylon" (Dan. 2:48). Seriously? Ruler over the whole province of Babylon? That's a pretty impressive leap forward. Quantum I would say.

The message for you and me is that in the uncomfortable moments we encounter, we must reject the default reaction to shy away and fall back into our comfort zone. "If you do what you've always done, you'll get what you've always gotten."[1] Being comfortable amounts to normal. And we don't want normal. We must learn how to be uncomfortable and to really embrace it. By doing the difficult things that are sometimes scary, we begin to notice huge gains. It is then that we are on the Way of the Warrior Saint.

ʃ PRACTICAL POINTS

Here are some practical points to help you implement being comfortable being uncomfortable. First, we have to remember that after a certain amount of repetition all new and scary things become easier. There is a beautiful Arabic maxim, *tikrar bi 'alam al-hamar*, which translates to "repetition taught the donkey." We learn to do new and difficult tasks ritualistically and habitually. Think I'm wrong? Remember how weird it was when you switched from a Microsoft computer to a Mac or vice versa? I grew up on Microsoft products. One day I made the decision to buy a MacBook. I was losing my mind dragging the cursor to the upper right corner to click the *X* to close a document. But there is no *X* on a

---

[1] Attributed to Henry Ford.

Mac. It's a small red circle. And it's in the upper left corner! At first it was frustrating. But after a certain period of time, my mind adapted. In fact, it became so well adapted to my Mac that now whenever I have to use a Microsoft product, I'm frustrated trying to find the small red circle in the upper left corner!

Most things actually work the same way, though at first, they might seem frightening or overwhelming. But by repetition, we begin to become comfortable with them. Running our first mile seems daunting until we're one month into daily running and are already at three miles. Giving a presentation to our boss or prospective clients is dreadfully uncomfortable until we've given the presentation fifty times and know it by heart. Asking a pretty girl out on a date can make even the strongest man sweat until he's asked—and perhaps been rejected by— numerous pretty girls to go to dinner. Having difficult conversations with co-workers or loved ones will make anyone squirm. But through a lot of practice, you can learn to embrace the hard conversations and handle them with love and gentility. The first practical point is to always remember that those things that make us uncomfortable become comfortable through time and repetition. Trust it.

Practical point number two puts practical point number one into action. Get out of bed earlier. Pretty simple. If you routinely wake up at 7:00 a.m., set your target for 6:00 a.m. tomorrow. I don't want you to applaud yourself because you did it for one day either. Make it the new normal. Getting up earlier is truly uncomfortable for most of us. We all want more sleep and the warm blankets put up a good fight. Set the target to get up one hour earlier for the next year. Yeah baby, let's get really uncomfortable! We're doing this experiment for a year! Not some easy gimmick test for thirty days. 365 days. I'm in. I am starting tomorrow. Let's do this.

Notice what's going to happen when you start getting up an hour earlier. First, you're going to feel ready to sleep earlier. I will never tell you to get up an hour earlier at the expense of an hour of sleep. We already don't get enough sleep. You need to keep the same amount of sleep time (or increase it) and your body will tell you that. There won't be many more 12:00 a.m. nights. You'll be out by 10:00 p.m. Second, you now have an hour in the morning to pray or do some quiet work. The world isn't totally functioning yet, but you are, so get some good work in. Most of this book was written in that newfound quiet hour. It might amaze you at some point how comfortable you'll become getting up an hour earlier. It will become a habit.

And our last practical point, I want you to actively seek out uncomfortable things to do. Let's not be dangerous. Just uncomfortable. Do you hate speaking in front of a large audience? Ask to give a presentation for your team. What about confronting that gal who's been talking about you behind your back? Ask for clarification as to why she's doing it. Afraid that you'll throw up if you continue to run so hard in your exercise? Puke anyway. Find some excitement in doing gnarly things! We're on the Way of the Warrior Saint. By definition, that implies a harder way—a way that sharpens iron against stone. Leave the normal people to do normal things and start being comfortable being uncomfortable.

Go get some.

2

TAKING RESPONSIBILITY

Jocko Willink is a retired Navy SEAL and was the commander of Task Unit Bruiser which served in Ramadi, Iraq in 2006. He was the leader on the ground in charge of putting down the insurgency in the fierce city of Ramadi. While preparing for one particular operation which he details in his book, *Extreme Ownership*, Jocko brought his SEALs together to share his battle plan. In the plan, his team was broken into four distinct SEAL units with snipers in each unit. With his fellow commanders, he drew up the plan of how they would assault the insurgency on that particular day. The local Iraqi army, though not as skilled or well-trained as the US Navy SEALs, were also on the mission as coalition forces. Once all of the preparations were complete, Jocko sent his team out into the city while he remained at headquarters to oversee the operation.

Using a powerful metaphor, Jocko describes how during the fog of war things never go as planned. No matter how tight the preparations, in the fog of war things can change quickly. And that night, one of his SEAL units began taking heavy fire from a fierce group of insurgents and were unable to reach their pre-planned coordinates. Taking cover in an adjacent building, the SEALs began to do what they're trained to do: fight. Being some of the most elite soldiers in the world, they brought thunder and lightning to the enemy outside the building.

At the very same time, another SEAL unit patrolling the main street was assaulted by the enemy from an elevated position in a nearby building. The insurgents fired at the SEALs relentlessly. The US Army support unit for the mission was forced to bring in a tank to deal with them. Before the end of that particular skirmish, one of the SEALs was seriously wounded, one of the Iraqi soldiers was killed and two others were hurt.

As happens to all good leaders in such a moment, Jocko got a funny feeling that something was not quite right. Leaving headquarters, he went to the battle site and discovered his worst fear: a blue-on-blue. Technically known as fratricide, a blue-on-blue means someone was killed by friendly fire. The SEALs that took cover inside the building were attacking the Army patrolling the main street outside. They were on the same team.

℘ TAKING RESPONSIBILITY IN CONTEXT

It can be frustrating when our plans don't work out like we hope. Many of us work hard to put out the best product we can. We don't always put in the requisite effort for success, but no one likes to come up short. Worse still is that when confronted with our mistakes the temptation is to direct blame somewhere else. Taking responsibility is a precious commodity that seems to be in short supply these days. During debrief at headquarters with all of his commanding officers present, with his job on the line and a terrible sadness for the blue-on-blue, Jocko had to figure out what went wrong. Somebody was responsible for the mix-up that cost soldiers their lives. But who was at fault? He asked his team that very question.

"Whose fault is this?" Jocko asked.

After a prolonged silence, one of the SEALs said, "Sir, it's my fault. I am the radio officer with the SEAL sniper team. I didn't radio our coordinates fast enough."

Jocko replied, "It's not your fault."

Another soldier said, "Sir, I was the SEAL that was assigned to be with the Iraqi unit. As they strayed from our plan, I didn't stop them. It's my fault."

"It's not your fault."

A third SEAL claimed responsibility. A fourth SEAL stood up, a fifth and a sixth. Each time Jocko said,

"Negative, it's not your fault." Then he did something most would consider insane. Jocko, looked at his men and said, "Do you know whose fault this is? It's my fault." Wait, what? Jocko's fault? He would be the last person to be responsible. He had drawn up tight battle plans and went through them with his team. During the fighting, it was the team that had strayed from those plans and ended up attacking each other. And for goodness sake, he wasn't even at the battle, so how could he be at fault?

Jocko took responsibility because that's what leaders do. He was the leading officer on the ground and was responsible for the outcome of the mission. In the fog of war, it would have been easy to throw blame elsewhere, but instead he held himself accountable. Jocko took responsibility for the death of the Iraqi soldier and the injuries sustained by his SEALs. He was a crucifixional leader.

Contrast this type of accountability with the system the world wants us to follow. Could you imagine taking that kind of responsibility? What if it meant risking your job and damaging your career? Or if it meant losing a relationship or perhaps even a spouse? What if taking responsibility meant that others would make fun of you? Would you still be willing to take responsibility?

The world likes when we make excuses. In making excuses and blaming others we become victims. We say things like: "It's too hard" or "I can't do it". Or we throw blame on another person. "It's my daddy's fault. He didn't love me enough. He didn't tell me all the things I needed to hear. He didn't make me feel good." Or, "It's my wife's fault. She nags me too much and stifles me from being the man I'm supposed to be." Or even, "It's my boss. He's after me. He doesn't want me to advance. When it's my turn for a promotion, he gives the other gal the nod instead of me." Do we even take responsibility for our health? "It's Marlboro's fault that I have lung cancer." Or, "I'm fat because of

McDonald's." We are more comfortable if we believe the system is out to get us and we allow ourselves to become victims. We become excuse-making victims. And victims have no control of their lives. I will delve more into that later.

❦ GOD'S INPUT

This is not a new phenomenon. It's not just you and me today who suffer from a failure to take responsibility and displace blame. From the beginning of time, the very first man was an excuse-making victim. In the opening chapters of the Book of Genesis we hear the story of the seven days of Creation when God created everything. The crowning moment is when God created Man and Woman and placed them in a paradisiacal garden. They were free to live and enjoy Paradise with only one caveat: there is a specific tree in the center of the garden, the Tree of the Knowledge of Good and Evil, and it was forbidden to touch. That's it. One tree among thousands that couldn't be touched. Of course, Adam not only touched the tree but also ate of its fruit! In the next part of the story, God came into the garden and questioned Adam, already knowing what he had done. God said to Adam,

"I know you ate from that tree. What do you have to say for yourself?"

At that moment, Adam faced a choice. He could man up and take responsibility or be an excuse-making victim. So, how did Adam respond?

"Well, the woman you gave me made me do it."

Boom. With one simple statement, Adam, in his failure to take responsibility, became an excuse-maker and a victim.[2] You and I face that question as well. If you're like me, you probably face it multiple times every day. Will I take responsibility or will I become an excuse-making victim? The entire point of the Adam and Eve story is to encourage us to not be like them. If only they had taken responsibility

---

[2] Our ladies shouldn't be too excited to rub that in. In the very next verse, Eve turns and blames the serpent for tricking her. See Genesis chapters 2-3 for the entire story.

for their actions, who knows how different the story could have been. Our success in life depends on how we answer that question. Being responsible for our own lives and our own actions is so essential to success that one could not be a Warrior Saint without it. So why do we so often end up taking the easy road and making excuses? Why are we so quick to default into excuse making? I think the answer is because we prefer to be comfortable. Remember in our previous chapter, "Being Comfortable Being Uncomfortable", we discovered that staying in our comfort zones is very easy to do. We don't have to face any fears, repercussions or embarrassments. We just default into the easier route and go about our day. We stay comfortable. And we stay mediocre.

Becoming great requires sacrifice. It requires being crucifixional. We have to face our fears and stand up to them. Sure, there will be consequences to every decision we make or fail to make, but those decisions are ours to make and we are therefore responsible for them. The funny part is, to that end, we want that responsibility. Yep, we actually want it, even if we say we don't. When we are constantly passing the blame—and therefore the responsibility—for our decisions elsewhere, we are also passing the control of our lives elsewhere. If other people or events are responsible for my decisions, they are in control of my actions. I go and do and say what other people dictate that I should go and do and say. In other words, I am not in control of my own life. And none of us want to be out of control. As we will see in a later chapter, I'd rather maintain control than relinquish control to someone else.

Taking responsibility is sometimes a painful thing to do. There's suffering and struggling that comes along with responsibility. And yet, Christ told us that the only way to follow Him to the empty tomb is through the Cross. The only way to raise life from the dead is through a crucifixional life. Do you want to be the man or woman you're supposed to be? Then you must embrace the hard way. You have to embrace the crucifixional life. You must embrace the suffering and embrace the struggle. By shunning the easy way, we find the success we're searching for. And that starts by actively seeking and accepting responsibility for as many decisions in your life as you can.

℘ PRACTICAL POINTS

So, if knowing that greatness begins by accepting responsibility, what steps can we take to implement a mindset of responsibility in our lives right now? I'm going to give you three suggestions. They're not exhaustive, but they're certainly three good ones with which to begin.

Our first practical point is to take care of ourselves. That means we begin by taking responsibility for our physical health. A later chapter on physical health will explore this idea more in depth, but suffice it to say, if you want to live long enough to be successful at your goals, you have to take your health seriously. Health isn't given for free. In fact, it is actually the opposite. If you take the easy road and do nothing, poor health will come for free. My promise to you: Doritos are not interested in your health. You must be interested in your health. You must take control. So, the first practical point to take control: run. And I mean run. I mean actually go outside into the outdoors and run. Run. And look, I know running isn't fun. I run every day and I never like it. Not once have I ever liked it. Not once during a run have I ever commented on how great it was. Never. It's hard. You're sweating and your body hurts. You're waging a war in your mind. You want to keep going but you want to quit even more. But something great happens when you're running. You know what you can't do while you're running? Eat a bag of Doritos.

Let's make it even harder. And better. Sometimes when you're running you may come to a fork in the road. You know that by turning left your run will total three and a half miles. You also know that by turning right your run will total four miles. Go for four. Don't cheat yourself out of greatness. It's harder, yes, but you can do it. Your body can do it. It is amazing what the human body can do if the mind would only get out of the way. And note, it doesn't have to be running, per se. Any type of exercise will help. You just have to get out there and get sweaty!

Our second practical point is to take responsibility for the next generation of Warrior Saints. I can think of nothing more important in this regard than to take responsibility for the education of our children.

You cannot honestly blame the world—or anyone else—for the mistakes of your children. They are ours to educate and no one else's. It's not okay for us to allow their teachers or the internet or their friends to educate them. We are blessed with children in order to teach them. Of course, our children attend school so their teachers can teach them math, science, English and other subjects. But what I'm talking about is teaching them a system of values, morality and a code of ethics. We cannot expect our children to become Warrior Saints by chance. It is our responsibility to teach them how to become Warrior Saints. The beginning of that is to impart to them a strong faith and moral compass.

So how might you do that? For starters, you can take your kids to church. I cannot tell you how many people I speak to who want their children to be faithful men and women but won't get out of bed on Sunday morning to bring them to church. Where else do you expect them to find the faith? And if you're not a Christian, that's okay. Take them to the services of your particular faith. Whatever your faith, don't pass that responsibility on to anyone else. This is especially important for men. All the pertinent data suggests young people's success is significantly higher when the father actively takes his children to church. Don't relinquish control to anyone, including your wife. "Honey, I've worked hard all week. You take them." Get up early, join your bride and take your kids to church! When you do so you are showing them what it means to be God-fearing men and women. And guess what? They will follow.

Our third and final practical point is to freely admit your mistakes. Jocko's story should be a powerful example for us. It would have been super easy for him not to say anything at all. His men were even taking responsibility at the start of his debrief. But he stepped up and took responsibility for himself, his team and the entire mission. By doing so, by not relinquishing control, he was able to make the following statement: "Yes, I failed, but I will make sure this never happens again." I wasn't a part of Task Unit Bruiser in 2006 and have no direct evidence, but my gut tells me that Jocko and his team did what they needed to do to ensure there was not another blue-on-blue during his tenure.

This is also particularly pertinent to men. As men, we're programmed to strive for perfection. Even in your formative years, how cool is it when your pee wee football team goes 6-0? A perfect season! Human DNA is wired to chase perfection and we do our best to maintain it. But the moment our perfect streak is broken, the temptation to default back into the easy way arises. Sadly, when this happens, we often deflect responsibility and pass the blame. But we've already seen that to pass the blame is also to pass control.

Instead, we have to admit our mistakes, accept the consequences of those actions and do everything within our power to ensure we don't repeat the same mistakes. To start that, you have to come to the realization that you will not be perfect. I know we like our perfect streaks of flawlessness, but they do not last. Ever. Something always pops up and throws us off our game. Yes, you are amazing and are able to do amazing things. In fact, I really believe that you can do just about anything you set your mind to. But you can't be perfect. So, let's begin by reminding ourselves that we are not going to be perfect.

Once we come to terms with our impending imperfection, our second task is to continually ask ourselves, "How did I fail in this situation?" By taking this approach, we are allowing ourselves to recognize that we are in control of the outcome of whatever decisions and actions we take. And even though we may have made poor decisions, we are still in control to correct them.

This leads to the last part of this practical point. Make a mental shift to look at each decision or action as a part of a greater whole. So, imagine that your goal is to accomplish x. Let's say the particular action y you took today didn't contribute to accomplishing x. Did you fail? In some sense, yes you did. And you should take full responsibility for y failing. But because x is your main goal and not y, it's not over yet! You still have time to accomplish x, and perhaps z is better suited to making that happen. You see therefore that by accepting responsibility for y doesn't mean we are a failure. It simply means that we tried something that didn't help in attaining x. What's the big deal with that? Just try something different to get to x. It's only when we're open to recognizing our mistakes that we will be free to try something new and better to accomplish our goals.

You may be wondering at this point how Jocko's story ended. Did his bold decision to take full responsibility end with him losing his job? Was he disgraced and kicked out of his SEALs team? Actually, quite the contrary. His commanding officers were so impressed with his responsibility that he not only kept his position, he remained in Iraq with his SEALs, helping the United States win the city of Ramadi. He served his country proudly and left the Armed Forces with a heavily distinguished career. Since his time in the Navy, Jocko has gone on to become a best-selling author, motivational speaker and high-demand business consultant. Learning from his story, it's clear that when control of our life is reclaimed by accepting responsibility for our actions, we can succeed like Jocko did.

Go get some.

3

HABITS

In the past few decades, scientific research surrounding habit formation has discovered that nearly fifty percent of our day-to-day actions are the product of habit. Once an action has become habitual, we rarely give it much thought. We subconsciously trust these mundane actions to habit, freeing our precious mental acuity to focus on more essential and exciting work. For example, I brush my teeth every morning, as I'm sure you all do, but I don't really think about it. I don't wake up and say, "I need to go to the bathroom and brush my teeth." Brushing my teeth is not on any of my to-do lists. In fact, on the occasional hectic morning, I've even had to return to the bathroom and check if the toothbrush was wet to make sure I did it. Without fail, I always found that my teeth were brushed. Brushing my teeth just sort of happens.

Habit is powerful and worth paying close attention to. An excellent text, *The Power of Habit*, delineates how powerful habits are and to what extent they impact our lives. The author Charles Duhigg has rightly intimated that something in control of almost half of our daily actions is worth looking at more deeply. I couldn't agree with him more. As Warrior Saints, we're supposed to be in control of every one of our actions. Therefore, if most of what we do is a product of habit, then it seems only reasonable that we should have some say in the habits that we allow to exist in our lives.

⸗ HABITS IN CONTEXT

You're probably familiar with the famous maxim attributed to Aristotle, "We are what we repeatedly do. Excellence, then, is not an act, but a habit." As we strive for excellence as Warrior Saints, it behooves us to take a quick look at how habits work. As you will see by the end of this chapter, in order to control what habits we allow to influence our lives, we must begin by understanding the process of habit formation.

Inside the human brain there are structures known as synapses. These tiny regions enable a neuron (a nerve cell) to transmit and receive electrical or chemical signals from other neurons. Connecting the millions of synapses in the human nervous system are fibrous nerve projections called axons. Axons can be imagined as little highways that the electrical impulses travel across from neuron to neuron. They are somewhat like roads that connect cities together. Electrical signals that follow a certain pathway of axons from neuron to neuron ultimately end up producing a thought or an action. One of the beautiful discoveries that science has made is that over time, when a specific synaptic pathway is used repeatedly, that pathway becomes so ingrained that "it just happens". In laymen's terms, a habit has been formed.

Think of it like this: one of the biggest habits that you and I engage in is checking our cell phone. The data is actually pretty frightening. Depending on which study you read, research claims that the average person interacts with their phone somewhere between 200 and 300 times a day. I don't do anything 200 times a day, so what makes my cell phone so alluring? Habit. Cell phones are designed to create habits in their users. When you hear the chime of a text message, a Facebook notification or an email coming in, what do you immediately do? You check the phone. When cell phones were new, it was super fun. But after time, we repeated the pattern so often that we became Pavlovian. Now, it just kind of happens. A new synaptic pathway has been created.

The new synaptic pathway always follows the same pattern. This pattern, what Duhigg refers to as a "habit loop," goes like this. First, there is a trigger or a cue that instigates the action. The cue hits our subconscious and reminds us to act. Next, a specific routine is followed.

Here, the actual action is taken. Finally, a reward is received for taking that specific action. That's the feel-good moment of a habit. To go back to the cell phone example, the notification chime is the cue, checking the phone is the routine and discovering the new information the phone is delivering is the reward. That's it. Cue, routine, reward. Repeated enough times, a new synaptic pathway is produced. A habit is born.

Research has also proven that once a synaptic pathway has been formed, it cannot be removed. That specific neural path will be with us until we die. This may sound like bad news for those trying to break a bad habit, but all hope is not lost. By the end of this chapter we will see that by being crucifixional, it is possible to take control of our habits.

ᔕ GOD'S INPUT

In 1 Corinthians, the Apostle Paul says, "All things are lawful for me, but not all things are helpful. All things are lawful for me, but I will not be enslaved by anything" (1 Cor. 6:12).

I love the freedom of this verse. In the specific context of chapter 6, Paul is talking about food restrictions, but there is a much deeper insight for us. He is teaching us that if something is helpful or beneficial or if there is a functional purpose for that thing in one's life, then it is okay to do it. If it will create good, if it will produce a positive outcome, go get some. However, we cannot allow ourselves to be enslaved to anything. He says, do not let anything be your master. Submit only to the Lord.

The word "enslaved" in this verse is translated from the Greek root *exousia*, which literally translates to "authority". Paul's message is that we cannot permit ourselves to be under the authority of anything that prohibits us from doing good. In the context of 1 Corinthians, he's talking about food specifically, but it can easily translate to any of our habits. Again, to return to our cell phone example, phones can be tremendously helpful. You can do so many things with your cell phone. But are we enslaved to them? Are we under the authority of the cell phone with all the imagery, sounds, notifications, requests and marketing that it pushes? That's a much deeper question because our phones use habit to enslave us. In a very real sense St. Paul is calling us to be in control of our habits. But as you know, habits are very hard to build and even harder to break. We are reminded of the saying, "old habits die hard." Is there a way to take control of our habits?

⸎ PRACTICAL POINTS

In his masterpiece of habit reform, *Atomic Habits*, author and blogger James Clear offers a treasure chest of steps one can take to gain control over habits. The three practical points in this chapter come directly from the research in his book. I highly recommend you read it.

First, Clear makes an astute observation that is good news for Warrior Saints. Though habit loops are permanently established in our brains, we don't necessarily have to submit to them. Would it be possible to use an old habit to create a new one? You bet it is. He calls it "habit stacking." For Clear, habit stacking means taking a currently existing habit and connecting to it the new, positive habit that you want to build. Imagine it being similar to tying a can to the bumper of a car. Wherever that car is going, it's going to pull the can along with it. Habit stacking allows the old existing habits to pull new and positive ones along with them.

As a trite but powerful example, nobody really likes to floss their teeth. Come on, admit it! I know most of us don't floss daily. It's a nuisance even though flossing is important for dental hygiene. And we all know that every time we go to the dentist, he's going to ask us why we're not flossing. He gives us those little samplers of dental floss and we promise to be diligent about it this time. We go our merry way only to throw the little samples in the back of the bathroom drawer where they remain out of sight and out of mind.

But what if we were to use habit stacking to become responsible flossers? That could be attempted like this. We know already that every day we brush our teeth. It's just something that happens. We don't think about it anymore. We don't search for the toothpaste, we don't search for the toothbrush, we don't write reminder notes. It just happens. It's a habit. What if for the next sixty days we stack our desired habit on top of the existing habit? At night, before you go to sleep, put your dental floss on top of your toothbrush. Now, every morning when you pick up your toothbrush, a habit that already exists, you are given a cue about the habit you're trying to build, which is the flossing. You can't get to the toothbrush until you at least acknowledge the little box of dental floss. By stacking your desired habit on top of an existing habit (literally!), you will have at least made the new habit accessible. Because you have to acknowledge the dental floss, it can become a cue for the new habit. It's true, you may choose to ignore the opportunity to floss your teeth, but at least it's not lost in the back of the drawer. It's physically present and the decision not to floss will at least be conscious. That leads us to the second practical point.

Use the environment to your advantage. Much of what we do is connected to a specific environment. Environment is a major cue for the habit loop. For example, the bathroom is where I brush my teeth. I don't go into the kitchen and think about brushing my teeth, but when I'm in the bathroom it just happens. So, use the environment to your advantage.

One of the habits that so many of us are trying to control is our enslavement to our cell phone. Every time we look at the phone, we are triggered to check what new notifications have come in. Every time it chimes, it is a cue to check and see who wants what. Control your environment. When you are trying to accomplish some deep work, turn the phone on silent mode. By doing so, you are removing the cue that starts the habit loop of engaging your phone.

A second tip you can use to control your environment is to put your phone somewhere you cannot see or hear it. It may seem funny, but consider hiding the phone from yourself when you want to focus on family, friends or work. If it's visible in your environment you will be tempted to look at it. If we're being totally honest with ourselves, the phone itself has become a cue. I know this to be a problem for myself. Every week I have a staff meeting with my team and I always put my phone in silent mode during that meeting. This allows me to give them my full and undivided attention. But when the phone is sitting on my desk, even in silent mode and even upside down, it's still physically present and is always pulling at my subconscious. The cue has been established and so no matter how much I want to focus on my team, the phone is always tickling the back of my mind. Instead, I have learned to control the environment and put the cell phone in a drawer. No cue, no bad habit.

Finally, the third practical point is to recognize that habits are neither easily nor quickly built. There is ample debate on how long it takes to build a new habit. I've heard it can take anywhere from twenty-one to sixty-six to ninety days to build a habit. I don't know what the actual answer is because I don't really think there is an answer. I think, however, the point is that something becomes a habit after we lose sight of it. So, how long does it take to lose sight of something? You should probably consider that answer to be never and therefore constantly work at controlling your habits. Building good habits is something you should be committed to for the rest of your life. Maintain your crucifixional attitude and sacrifice the comfort of falling back into old patterns, and I promise you positive change is waiting for you right around the corner.

Go get some.

4

PHYSICAL HEALTH

I was assigned to serve as pastor of St. George Antiochian Orthodox Church in Phoenix, Arizona in December 1999. In the first sixty days we were there, my bride and I spent five nights at home. Our parish family was so gracious and invited us to dinner for fifty-five of the first sixty nights we were there! Hospitality being their specialty, we were treated like royalty. We got quality time with the people we would be serving in the intimate setting of their family homes. It was some of the most foundational work we did for our future service to them. The best part of all was that they served some of my favorite meals. Of course, you can't say no to someone's hospitality, so I got to eat!

Those first few months we spent countless hours learning the local traditions of the parish, the layout of where our people lived and worked within the city and what the needs of the community were. We worked tirelessly day and night to serve them to the best of our ability. My bride was on her way to work by 6:30 a.m. and I was in the shower right behind her. We arrived home after 10:00 p.m. most nights, just in time to catch a few hours of sleep before we woke up the next day to get back after it.

℘ PHYSICAL HEALTH IN CONTEXT

Human beings are neither a body nor a soul. We are both body and soul. Perhaps that's what separates us from animals and makes us in the image of God. Though it is essential to nourish our souls in order to draw ever closer to a fully crucifixional life, we cannot neglect our bodies. There is an intimate connection between our bodies and our souls and any neglect of one adversely affects the other. The hard work we did upon arrival in Phoenix was solely dedicated to feeding the soul. My lifestyle for the first sixty days in the parish focused on others at the expense of healthy eating, exercise and sleep. It didn't take long before I started feeling the effects of this lifestyle. When I left seminary in 1998, I was wearing pants that were waist-sized 32. By mid-2000 I had to buy pants sized 40. No joke. I didn't even look like myself. I was puffy and bloated. My mind typically races along, but I felt groggy all the time and couldn't think clearly. My sleep was suffering, as was my ministry.

Thankfully, my doctor was a member of the parish and he noticed my transformation. He asked me numerous times to come in for a check-up, but in my typical machismo, I said, "Nah, I'm fine." Until one night while driving home from dinner at a parishioner's house, I reflexively unbuckled the belt on my pants to relieve some of the pressure. It hit me like a ton of bricks. Am I so overweight that I have to unbuckle my pants to get comfortable? Sadly, the answer was yes.

So, I finally accepted my doctor's invitation and went in for a check-up. As it turned out, it was a good thing I did. Not only was my waist size 40, I now weighed 205 pounds and my cholesterol was 317. For a twenty-nine-year-old man who measures 5'9" on a good day, you can imagine what I looked like. And I bet some of you can imagine what I felt like. After scolding me properly, the doctor wrote a prescription for cholesterol medication. I was devastated that I was now being forced to take a pill every day for the rest of my life. There had to be another way. Doc said, "Sure, diet and exercise." It was on.

In our fast-paced world where time is so precious and so elusive, it is easy to become physically unhealthy like I was. Fat, sick and stressed, I was not a great version of myself. I wanted to do better but when would I have the time? If you feel like I did, then you know the pressures of trying to do it all. Eating fast food in your car, unable to run a mile and trying to keep up to the demands of your overpacked schedule.

Warrior Saints are called to be a little different. A lot different, actually. Our bodies are gifts and it is our responsibility to take care of them, not for the sake of vanity but for the sake of making our highest offering to the world. To be great, we have to be healthy.

ꕔ GOD'S INPUT

In 1 Corinthians, the Apostle Paul uses the metaphor of the human body to speak about the church community he founded in that city. In chapter 6 we hear, "Do you not know that your body is a temple of the Holy Spirit within you, which you have from God?" (1 Cor. 6:19).

This is a fabulous text in which the Apostle is calling his community to correct behavior. In this specific verse, the phrase "within you" is in the third person plural. That means he is not talking about any one specific person's body but the entire body of the church community. I was born in West Virginia. We would say it means "you" as in "all y'alls." That means that the body that the Holy Spirit dwells within is not an individual, but the larger body of the fledgling Church community.

However, just a few verses earlier, St. Paul asks the Corinthian Christians if they know that, "their bodies are members of Christ?" (1 Cor. 6:15). Here he is speaking to each person directly and individually. Each person is an individual member of the larger Body of Christ. He is exhorting them not to submit their own physical bodies to wickedness so that they can be a fully healthy contributing member to the larger body: their church. In order to have a healthy body, each member has to be in tip-top shape. The same holds true for you and me. If we're going to make an impact in the world and be contributing members of our communities, we have to begin by taking care of our own individual bodies. That means we've got to be healthy.

Before we get to the practical points, let's take a quick excursus and explore our personal value to the community. So often many of us feel like we don't really matter or that our contribution is lesser than others and therefore of no value. Feeling like that, it's easy to default to drive-through windows, overpacked schedules and only exercising by thumbing the remote control.

But you do matter. You are important even if you don't think so. Think of it like the pinky toe. Scientists and medical researchers are convinced that the pinky toe is evolving away. We don't need it for balance or walking or climbing. In generations to come, it will eventually disappear from the human body. Ultimately, the pinky toe appears to be without value for the human being. But tell me what happens when you stub your pinky toe? You know like that time you walked by the end table without your shoes on and caught the bottom of the table leg just close enough to snag the pinky toe and nearly tear it from your foot. Did you laugh it off? Of course not. The pain is excruciating. Your entire body writhes in pain. If you're like me, you grab your foot and hop around on one leg massaging the injured toe. You do that because no matter how insignificant the pinky toe may seem, it is a part of the body and when it suffers the entire body suffers. You're the same. You are a part of the larger body of your community. Your family, your work, your church, your city, the world. You are a part of a body larger than yourself and when you are suffering so does the whole body.

And so, you see it is our responsibility to take care of ourselves no matter how difficult it may seem. We must take responsibility, not so that we can look svelte in our bathing suits at the beach, but so that we can live as long and as healthy a life as possible. Death is surely coming for us all, but that doesn't mean we need to hasten its arrival. We all have something to offer and it's our job to make sure we're around to do so.

I am not a nutritionist nor a medical doctor and I never want to lead someone astray. I encourage you to meet with your health professionals and maintain regular contact with them. They will be your ultimate guides toward good health. My only caution is to be wary of any health professional that wants to give you a magic pill to fix your health. If there were such a magic pill the health industry wouldn't be as large a machine as it is. To be healthy requires being crucifixional. We're going to have to suffer a little bit, get off the couch, eat the right things and put in the work. That leads us to our practical points.

℘ PRACTICAL POINTS

Our first practical point is to control what goes into your mouth. I firmly believe that ninety percent of physical health is connected to what you eat. The body is a machine and it needs the proper fuel to function at its highest level. If you are overloading your body with toxins, you can't expect it to function well. Just as a performance car needs higher octane gasoline to run at optimal levels, so too do our bodies need good fuel to be at our best.

Quite frankly, so much of what we eat today is toxic. I've become a label reader, meaning I read the labels of the foods I consume. I want to see what's in the food I'm about to eat. It's shocking how much of our food contains ingredients that have more than ten letters in their name and are barely pronounceable. It's no wonder that we don't feel good as a society. The fuel we're putting into our bodies isn't helping us as much as it's hurting us. As I mentioned, I am not a nutritionist nor a medical doctor, but it seems pretty clear that if we can't pronounce it, we probably shouldn't be eating it.

Instead put high-quality, clean food into your body and follow the guidance of your medical professionals. There are a few things we can be sure are detrimental to our health. Sugar has to be on top of that list. There are countless studies that illustrate the harmful effects of sugar. Some research has even compared the addictiveness of sugar to that of cocaine and heroin and has discovered that it affects the brain in similar fashion. Sugar has been compared to super-stimuli that produces a release of dopamine (like cocaine) and also disrupts the opioid pathways (like heroin) in the brain. Researchers Daniel Blumenthal and Mark Gold conclude that this disruption contributes to the inability to control consumption.[3] In other words, once you start eating sugar, it's hard to stop. Like I said at the beginning of the book, I either eat no Doritos or I eat all the Doritos! Please let me say that I'm not suggesting we never consume sugar again. That would be nigh on impossible and no fun. I love taking my family out for ice cream on warm summer nights. I'm simply reminding you to be crucifixional and take control of what goes in your mouth. You cannot live a long, healthy and productive life if you are not in control of your diet.

I also suggest you control your consumption of alcohol. Look, I am no prude who thinks any alcohol consumption is evil. There are well known health benefits from drinking certain types of alcohol in moderation. I enjoy a glass of bourbon with a cigar on my patio to end the day. I relish that time talking with my family or even watching a Lakers' game. When used properly, alcohol is not inherently bad. Even the Bible tells us that God "caused grass to grow for cattle and **wine to make glad the heart of man**" (Ps. 104:14-15, emphasis mine).

The problem with alcohol is that it causes everything to start shutting down. What I mean is, contrary to what many people use alcohol for, alcohol is actually a depressant that slows down brain function. Classified as a central nervous system depressant, alcohol slows down brain functioning and neural activity by enhancing the effects of the neurotransmitter gamma-aminobutyric acid (GABA)[4]. GABA is an amino acid that functions as a neurotransmitter in our brain and exists to inhibit neurotransmission. In layman's terms this means that GABA slows down the transmission of messages between brain cells. In normal healthy human beings, GABA is an essential part of a healthy mind. Without GABA, the nerve cells would fire with little to inhibit them and nerve transmissions would increase. Think about what coffee does to us. Caffeine inhibits GABA and we

---

[3] https://pubmed.ncbi.nlm.nih.gov/20495452/ Also see: https://www.healthline.com/nutrition/10-similarities-between-junk-foods-and-drugs#section1. *This article is a concise overview that cites numerous reputable studies.*

[4] See for example: https://www.addictioncenter.com/alcohol/is-alcohol-a-depressant/

"wake up."[5] An oversaturation of GABA produces the opposite effect. Neurotransmissions are less frequent, or cease all together, producing a sensation of calm or relaxation. Alcohol use enhances the effect of GABA and gives its user the feeling of relaxation.

For this Warrior Saint, that means the end of any productivity for the balance of the day. For example, if I come home in the evening and I want to prepare a lecture or do research on a specific topic but decide to have a glass of bourbon to unwind before I do so, I may as well drink the whole bottle of bourbon. I'm not getting anything done! Once that feeling of relaxation starts setting in, it's difficult to fight and make any productive contribution to my mission.

And you know what else slows down? The ability to say no. Long has alcohol been linked with poor decision making and rightfully so. We all know that person—or may even have been that person—who has made some awful choices under the influence of alcohol. As Warrior Saints who, in this chapter are focusing on physical health, alcohol quickly inhibits the willpower to say no to snacking. Imagine that you've spent all day eating healthy and you even woke up early to exercise. You want to put this day in the books as a win. You celebrate with a small drink and a cigar on your patio. And then you see them. The cookies your girls just baked. Sitting on the counter cooling down and calling your name. It's not an easy battle to win under the best of circumstances, but it's even more difficult under the influence of alcohol and with an increase in GABA! Your day is no longer a win. It's a total bust. When under the influence of alcohol, remember your ability to say no to the harmful choices —or at least less healthy ones—drops drastically. You have to be crucifixional and take control of your alcohol consumption.

Our second practical point is to control your daily activity level. That means that you have to make sure you get sweaty every single day. Though diet is by far the largest factor in physical well-being, exercise cannot be overlooked. There are so many positive outcomes from exercise, the first of which is increased energy levels. I don't know about you, but after a good run, you know, the kind where you're totally

---

[5] http://www.chm.bris.ac.uk/motm/gaba/gabajm.htm

dripping with sweat, I'm ready to take on the rest of the day. I'm firing on all cylinders after a good sweat. The second part of a good sweat is clarity of mind. With the proverbial juices flowing after a great workout, I think so much clearer, so much faster and so much deeper. Some of my best work has been done during a workout or immediately following one. I also find it easier to handle whatever may come my way each day. Getting sweaty won't change the obstacles you have to face each day. However, it changes the way you look at those obstacles. A fresh, sharp mind is better equipped to face the challenges that life presents us. Lastly, a good sweat will help you sleep better at night.

That leads to our third practical point: you have to control your sleep. Prevailing science today is unanimous in its conclusion that sleep is essential to our physical and mental well-being. Nearly all scientific research shows that to maintain a healthy life we need a minimum of seven to eight hours of sleep a night. The days of sleeping less in order to work more have been thoroughly debunked. It is clear that the less sleep one gets the lower the quality and quantity of work one can produce, even if more time is spent working. The correlation between hours worked and quality of work drops significantly when sleep drops below optimal levels. It is imperative that we take our sleep seriously if we want to maintain a healthy lifestyle.

We're going to have to make a lot of sacrifices to get proper sleep. It's easy to stay up late binge-watching Netflix or playing *Call of Duty*. Being a Warrior Saint takes a lot more discipline and a crucifixional attitude. First, we have to get up early. Not everyone likes getting up early. I sure don't. But our best work gets done when it's quiet and distraction free. Certainly, some people do their best work in the afternoon hours, but the majority of us think clearer early in the day before our willpower has been taxed. And waking up earlier helps us go to sleep earlier. Develop a pattern of going to sleep at the same time each day. Our bodies crave rhythm and that includes the rhythm of sleep. When we get used to the habit of sleeping at a specific time, our bodies know that it's time to shut down for the day.

Another trick to aid sleeping at the same time each day is to limit your screen time before sleep. Sleep disorders specialist, Harneet Walia,

MD, sheds some light on this sleep-sabotaging habit. In agreement with the prevailing research, Dr. Walia says that we should put our screens down at least one hour prior to sleep.[6] The blue light of your cell phone has been shown to imitate natural light which is a signal for our bodies to get up and face the day. I also suggest watching your caffeine intake after lunch. Everybody is different, so I recommend spending some time experimenting to learn when your caffeine cut-off time should be.

Remember Warrior Saints, your body is a gift, a machine to enable you to make a contribution to the world. You've got the responsibility to keep it in tip-top shape so that your contribution is not good but great. To be great, you have to be healthy. To be healthy, you have to take care of the machine.

Go get some.

---

[6] https://health.clevelandclinic.org/put-the-phone-away-3-reasons-why-looking-at-it-before-bed-is-a-bad-habit/#:~:text=closer%20to%20bedtime.-,Dr.,can%20contribute%20to%20poor%20sleep

5

FIGHTING MONSTERS

We often assume that monsters are mythical and magical beasts reserved only for the movies and wonderful fantasy tales. Tolkien's Middle Earth in *The Lord of the Rings* trilogy, for example, so vividly opens our imagination to a world of trolls and Uruk-hai and wizards and elves and dragons. The power the monsters possess is seemingly unconquerable. The fear our heroes face often makes them question their strength and initial desire to embark on their mission. The heroes in our favorite stories face impossible odds and yet are still expected to save the world and all of mankind. Some of them are given special powers to fight against the monsters. And some of them are given guides—masters if you will—to show them how to use those superpowers. But in the end, they are always victorious through a lot of hard work, self-sacrifice and a touch of luck. (I mean, come on, how could the Stormtroopers always have such bad aim?!) But fighting monsters is reserved for fantasyland. Since monsters don't actually exist, I don't have to be worried about facing them. I mean, I'm not Gandalf and there's no Balrog in the path of my life.

But is that entirely true? Are there really no monsters to fight? Do we live in a world that is free from evil and struggle and anger and suffering and ferocious attacks? If we're honest with ourselves and truly examine our hearts and minds, I think we'll find that there are indeed many fearsome monsters to fight and conquer. Coming in different flavors, they may be more numerous than we could imagine. They may not be winged dragons but they are certainly just as real and terrible.

℥ FIGHTING MONSTERS IN CONTEXT

Anxiety, fear, depression, anger, suffering, drugs and alcohol, marital strife, troubled children, poor physical health, cancer, divorce, feeling stuck and trapped, debt, hunger, gossip, not having enough time, not having enough money, not making enough money, feeling like the world is pressing down upon you and constantly squeezing the life out of you, feeling like you have so much more to offer to the world, having no direction, doubt, lack of motivation, questioning one's self-worth, political fighting, a bad boss, bad co-workers, bad employees, a bad economy, hate…

I could go on and on with this list. My guess is that you fight with some of the above and could also add your own to this list of monsters. The truth is, they are just as real as fantasy monsters. And we are at war with them in our lives every day. And we often wonder if it is a war that we're destined to lose.

If our heroes of old taught us anything, it's that deep within us, maybe even buried way below the surface of our consciousness, there is a greatness lying dormant. It is a greatness that is screaming to get out, to be turned loose on the world and to conquer our monsters. G.K. Chesterton said that, "[f]airytales are more than true; not because they tell us dragons exist, but because they tell us that dragons can be beaten." We may not believe that sometimes. We have all gone through those moments where our monsters seem unconquerable. It's not uncommon to doubt ourselves. But I beg you to take confidence in God that He put the power to defeat our monsters deep within us.

℥ GOD'S INPUT

So how do we conquer our monsters? Simple. We conquer them by living a life of the Cross or, as we mentioned before, what Warrior Saints call crucifixional living. As we noted in the introduction, the greatest monster of all time is Death. Because it is beyond humanity's ability to conquer, God sent His only Son, Jesus Christ, to do battle with the great monster on our behalf. Through His voluntary death on the Cross, Jesus did indeed destroy the power of Death. As counterintuitive as it may seem, Death was trampled down by death.

In a stunning twist, the writers of the Gospels reveal that Jesus personally invites us to face and conquer our own monsters in the exact same manner. In the Gospel of Mark, we hear that invitation:

> "And He called to Him the multitude with His disciples, and said to them, 'If any man would come after Me, let him deny himself and take up his cross and follow Me. For whoever would save his life will lose it; and whoever loses his life for My sake and the gospel's will save it,'" (Mark 8:34-35).

Here, Christ is saying to us that the world tells you to "get yours" in order to conquer monsters. But we all know that doesn't work. The only way to truly conquer the monsters you face is to live a life of the Cross. Just as He conquered the greatest monster of all time on the Cross, so too can you conquer your monsters—whatever they may be—by imitating Christ and living a crucifixional life.

Many doubt this truth. Instead of denying the self, the world is encouraging you to find comfort and fulfill all your desires. "You do you." The power of crucifixional living even seems to have escaped the Apostles. In one instance during a journey from Jerusalem to a town called Emmaus, two of Jesus' followers expressed deep regret for His Crucifixion. They had hoped that He was "the one to redeem Israel." In their minds, He was supposed to live, rally the troops and expel the Roman occupiers in the same manner an earthly king would expel invaders. Christ approached them and joined the discussion. Upon hearing their doubt, He uttered, "O foolish men, and slow of heart to believe all that the prophets have spoken! **Was it not necessary that the Christ should suffer these things and enter into His glory?**" (Luke

24:25-26, emphasis mine). It's as if He is saying, don't doubt the truth of the Cross; through the adversity of a crucifixional life, you will enter into glory.

ℰ PRACTICAL POINTS

"Yeah," you might say, "easy for Jesus. He is the Son of God after all." Yes, He is. But don't sell yourself short. You've got a little bit of that glory inside you, too. In Genesis, the first book in the Bible, we hear that man is "made in the image and likeness of God," (Gen. 1:26). The interpretation of that verse can be a conversation for another time, but the point is that you have greatness inside. Somehow, the very image of God is inside each and every one of us. We may not have nourished it and we may have let it lie dormant. We may have even helped stifle it. But it's there nonetheless. And our challenge—nay, our opportunity— is to set it free, to unlock the greatness within us and conquer our monsters. I know you can do it. I believe in you even though I don't know you. I believe in you because I believe that the divine spark is in you, in all of us, and I want to help you turn it loose.

So where do we begin? We begin by first believing that God did indeed stamp you with His image. This is not simply a belief in a magical type of god that floats in the clouds using his magic wand to make you special or make you look like mankind in Michelangelo's famous painting, The Creation of Adam. It's something much deeper than that. It is believing that you matter. You are of great value and have been given gifts that can make an impact on the world. Every single one of you, no matter how insignificant you may think you are, has some awesome in you. This isn't to say we need to get carried away and lost in our ego—that wouldn't be crucifixional at all—but it's to start from the position that you are not useless. You are not a loser. If you have the desire to succeed and combine it with grit, you can find your great and set it free. It's in you and you have to take confidence in that. Believe it.

I'm not anything special. Really, I'm not. I'm just some dude who felt like my gift was to share this teaching with the world. But I'm not a writer. I loathe it in fact. More than that, I was afraid that people would read my thoughts and my words and hate them and by extension hate me. I was afraid that people would make fun of what was in my mind and I would become the laughingstock of the book-writing world. And then it hit me. One day someone said powerful words that changed my life: "God made you, so believe in yourself. You just have to trust in Him and share your mind with the world." You're reading this book right now because of those words. I trusted those words and dug deep inside to fight my dread of writing and produce this work. And you know what? It was hard. Totally hard. And some people may hate this book and hate me and make fun of me. And that's okay, because I found within me something that I didn't know I had. I became a book writer. You can begin to believe in yourself too.

Below are some very simple and practical steps you can implement right now to start believing in yourself. First, don't stress out! You may think you have a long way to go to find greatness and that can be overwhelming. That's usually the case for most of us. Most of us don't start out great. We have to move towards greatness, constantly grinding every day. But because we're not where we want to be, and we see that where we want to be is super far away, we get intimidated by the distance of the journey and talk ourselves out of taking any steps towards it. It seems so overwhelming that we let the distance scare us out of even trying and sit stagnant and steeped in our mediocrity. The first step is to stay focused and remember that everyone started where you are. Even the great ones.

Second, what if you were to try moving forward by only a small margin today? Let's say obesity is your fiercest monster and losing forty pounds is your goal. What if you just decide not to eat Doritos today? That's it! Just don't eat Doritos today. Nothing else in your life changes, just the Doritos. That's it. In the grand scheme of things, you probably won't lose those forty extra pounds by eating no Doritos today. But something else happens. It's a small win. One small win. One thing that you can look back at the end of the day and say, I didn't eat Doritos today! What do you think you might want to do tomorrow? If you're like me, you'd want to repeat that Doritos fast. And now you have two days. And then three. And four. And soon you have a streak going. One small win can quickly multiply in your mind and then confidence sets in. I suggest getting a calendar of some kind, whether an app on your phone or a big wall calendar. Each day you don't eat Doritos put a big X on that date. There is science behind the psychology of seeing a visual streak. It is said to have been an integral part of Jerry Seinfeld's joke-writing career. Seinfeld reportedly wrote a joke every day, and when he did, he got to put a big red X on his calendar. He became so attached to the streak that he didn't want to break it. So, he kept writing jokes every day. It seems to have worked for him.

I know it works for me. I use a Fitbit to track my daily steps and exercise. Every day that I exercise, I get a star for working out. Every day I hit my step goal, I get a star for 10,000 steps. I absolutely hate breaking a streak of stars. And so, every day I work out and get my steps. At this point, it's about the streak not the exercise!

The next thing you know, that streak flows over into other areas of life. Maybe you've added exercise to your daily regimen. Now you're not only avoiding Doritos but you're doing ten minutes of walking each day. And soon it becomes twenty minutes and then it becomes thirty minutes and then it's a light jog and a run and a sprint. Dietary changes follow and you've stopped eating processed foods. And then sugar. And then all of a sudden, forty pounds doesn't look so daunting. And you're becoming a lion. You're gonna get it. And it all started by skipping a snack-sized Doritos bag at lunch. In essence, all you did was make a one percent change in your life. That's it. One percent.

I call this the *One Percent Rule*. If I can just change a habit by one percent, the effects over time can be staggering. What makes it so cool is that I hardly notice the one percent change while I'm doing it. Because it's so small, it doesn't have that fear-inducing quality and I can quickly overlook it. It may even go totally unnoticed. Remember Aristotle's quote? "We are what we repeatedly do. Excellence, then, is not an act, but a habit."[7]

---

[7] There is debate over whether Aristotle actually said this or not. See for example Durant, W. *The Story of Philosophy: The Lives and Opinions of the World's Greatest Philosophers.* (1926) New York: Simon & Schuster, revised edition 1933. Regardless of who said it, the point should be pretty clear.

So, the first step towards great is believing that greatness is within you. It's there and you just have to unlock it. Set it free. The second step is the *One Percent Rule*. Just get one percent better today than you were yesterday. Two simple steps and that's it.

Go get some.

6

THE TEACUP AND THE LION

You remember those pretty little teacups in the china cabinet that your mother or grandmother would bring out for guests during formal holiday dinners? You know, the ones that were often ornate and beautiful in design. They were the ones that reminded you of the grandeur of elegance and nobility. And they were usually the ones that only the adults were able to drink from because they were so fragile. (You may have even learned this firsthand!) Their delicate handles could snap off and chips could happen easily. Even the slightest contact with a hard surface and the entire cup would shatter.

Now, let's compare that fragility to a moniker bestowed upon today's younger generations: teacup. And just as that lovely china cabinet protects actual teacups from damage, we now too have a generation of parents – dubbed helicopter parents – who likewise hover over their delicate offspring in an attempt to safeguard them from any potential difficulties which life may throw at them. Like the teacups' fragile namesake, many young people are easily shattered when making contact with any hard surface in their world. Being offended is the trendy thing to do right now. We build safe spaces on high school and college campuses, H.R. departments have redesigned proper office protocol and created sensitivity training, anxiety medication is prescribed liberally. It seems to have become inherently necessary to protect people, especially men, from other people. The thought process seems to be that by insulating people from offensive and hurtful remarks, ideas and words, they will be better for it.

Unfortunately, the outcome of this flawed reasoning is a generation of people in a constant state of fear. It breaks my heart to see them constantly looking over their shoulders and never knowing what will be the next trigger. It has also produced a new police force. Social justice warriors or progressives—whatever you want to name them—spend an inordinate amount of time telling people how to act, what to say and what to think. This is all done in the name of protecting the teacups. But now we have created monsters that have no choice but to shatter.

The desire to protect our children and the less fortunate from painful experiences usually has only one motivator which is love. We love our children and want to see them safe and happy and laughing. No one wants to see their children suffer. No wants to see weaker people being oppressed. We love them and want to protect them. The problem with overprotecting people is the inevitability of producing teacups. Even though the motivation is love, the outcome is a life of constant fear.

၌ THE TEACUP AND THE LION IN CONTEXT

I remember very clearly the day when my cousin called to tell me his son had just eaten his first clump of dirt. It was a glorious day for my godson. Though not yet able to walk, he was an active and energetic young child. That day, as he was crawling around in the backyard, he found a clump of dirt and did what every infant would do. He ate it.

Some may consider that gross, and it's true that eating dirt isn't the best source of protein, but it's an indicator of something deeper. It showed me that my cousin and his wife were not afraid to let him explore, get dirty and bang up against some rough edges. He was allowed to face difficult things. Sure, he'd have skinned knees and broken arms and hurt feelings, but he'd be a better man because of those experiences. And as I write this chapter, he is a few months away from graduating high school. I have watched him grow since his dirt-clump-eating days, and he is one of the finest—and fiercest—young men I know. As he prepares to attend college next year, I have no doubt that he will be successful in whatever he endeavors to do in his life. That young man is no teacup. He's becoming a lion.

We are meant to face hard things in order to overcome them. I'm convinced that so much of the recent surge in diagnosed depression is directly connected to the attempt to remove challenges and pain in our world, especially among young men. We expect—nay, we crave—challenges and suffering and work. Doing the hard things actually reveals the character of the man. To keep us from those challenges does us all a great disservice.

Think of it like this. Do you remember that time when you took a little hiatus from the gym and your return was a bit painful? You know, the day after leg day and every muscle in your lower body was in pain? So much so that it was hard to walk up the stairs or even to sit down. The reason you felt that pain is attributed to something called delayed onset muscle soreness (DOMS). After a particularly hard work-out or a work-out where you tried some new exercises, your muscles experience micro-tears in the fibers. Cells are dying and being replaced with new cells to heal the micro-tears. They are replaced by bigger and stronger cells. We all certainly waddle around after leg day complaining about the pain. But it's a good pain. I love that pain. It means I did something difficult and came out on the other side a little bit better. Notice too how after a relatively short period of time, the post workout pain seems to vanish. It's like our body acclimates to the strenuous activity. That's because it does. You've broken down some of the weaker cells in the fibers of your muscles and the new cells grew back bigger and stronger and more able to handle the stress of the workout.

The same is true for our egos. If we allow ourselves or our children to be exposed to challenging things, we start to grow into stronger and more solid men and women. Yes, we will fail and get hurt and get offended, but we'll move on. The cells of our moxie will grow back bigger and stronger. We're on our way to becoming Warrior Saints. Lions, not teacups.

Ⅎ GOD'S INPUT

The story of Job is a powerful tale of a man who had everything taken from him. Living in the land of Uz, Job was blessed with seven sons and three daughters. He had thousands of camels, sheep, oxen and she-asses, indicating that he was a man of great wealth. He had more servants working in his house than anyone of his day. All of these blessings were given to Job because he feared God, led a blameless and upright life and always turned away from evil (Job 1:1-3). Early on in the text, Satan approached God with a proposition and test: allow him to thrust misfortune and hardship on Job. Satan was sure that when Job was confronted with the most challenging of times, he would renounce God. It was kind of like a teacup test.

In the story, God gave Satan permission to run his little experiment, and therein a horror story of sadness ensued. Enemies and firestorms destroyed all of Job's animals, servants and property. A great wind blew across the wilderness which knocked down his house and killed all ten of his children. Shortly thereafter, Satan infected Job with a great plague of sores all over his skin. Utterly shattered, all that remained to him was his wife and his faith in God.

But was he really shattered? Was he a teacup smashed against the rigidity of his life's events? The message of the Book of Job is ultimately a resounding example of how to overcome the brittle nature of teacups. His wife and his three best friends tried to persuade Job to curse God and be done with it. And yet, in spite of all of the suffering, all of the temptation and all of the hardship, Job never cursed God. He remained steadfast to the end. He confronted the difficulties of life—in his case, extreme difficulties—but did not shatter. In so doing, he personified what we would call a Warrior Saint in action. When confronted with difficulty, Warrior Saints do not waver and they do not break.

Something beautiful happened at the end of the story. All of Job's suffering was washed away and everything that he previously lost was restored. He regained his wealth with twice as many cattle as he lost. He had twice as many servants as before. He was even blessed with new children. A literal reading may be far-fetched, but that's okay. We're more interested in the meaning of the story. Job teaches us that in times of great difficulties we must maintain a ferocious faith, intent on never shattering against hardship. In so doing, we can become twice the person we were when we started. The power to do so resides inside each one of us. As we hear at the end of the book, when you stand strong for God, "[t]hen will I also acknowledge to you, that your own right hand can give you victory," (Job 40:14).

℥ PRACTICAL POINTS

Let's explore three practical points to help us become strong and anti-fragile. Our first practical point is simple but very hard: ignore an offensive person. Just ignore them. They are hurling the offense at you to get a rise out of you. When you get offended by them, you have given them exactly what they want. The Book of Proverbs says that "[f]ools show their annoyance at once, but the prudent ignores an insult," (New International Version, Prov. 12:16). As we're trying to overcome the *Teacup Syndrome,* we have to realize that offensive people actually exist in the world. That's right, offensive people do exist and we're going to encounter them. And they're probably going to offend us at some point. And what's the big deal? So what if someone said something offensive? That's what offensive people do. They say offensive things. But you know what never happened because someone said something offensive? Death. That's right. Offensive remarks can't kill you. I understand that offensive remarks don't feel good to our egos, but we're trying to become lions not fragile teacups. Lions don't really pay much attention to what the sheep say. They just ignore them and then eat them. Big deal someone made an offensive remark. Just ignore it. Only fools care about what others say.

A quick addendum to our first practical point is in order. If we're honest with ourselves, it may very well be that we deserve the offensive remark. Maybe you actually did something—inadvertently or not—to hurt another person. And maybe in their inability to forgive they responded by lashing out with offensive remarks. Be a little bit crucifixional, endure the offense and apologize for your actions. You'll be better in the end because of it.

Our second practical point is to show a little compassion to the person throwing offensive remarks around. Remember, broken people say broken things. Be crucifixional and have a little compassion for the suffering they may be going through. "Good sense makes one slow to anger, and it is his glory to overlook an offense," (Prov. 19:11). Maybe there is tragedy in an offensive person's life and they are simply purging their frustration on the world. Perhaps you just happened to be the recipient of that frustration. It's not fun for sure, but we're seeking crucifixional lives and it's our responsibility to sacrifice a little bit of ourselves for the sake of another person. Instead of reacting quickly in anger, take a breath and respond with something nice. I promise you, nine times out of ten you will diffuse the situation immediately. And perhaps the other person may realize what he or she said and apologize!

Our final practical point is to remember that very few things truly matter. In our 24/7, 365 days-a-year news culture, mountains are constantly being made out of mole hills. The media has to do that in order to fill the space. It's got to be hard to have breaking news every hour of every day. But that doesn't mean we have to buy it. Don't give credence to things that don't deserve it. "There is no remembrance of former things, nor will there be any remembrance of later things yet to happen among those who come after," (Eccl. 1:11). Just because someone tells you something is important doesn't mean it actually is. It is your responsibility to decide what is truly important to you. Consider the things that really matter and fight for those. My bride is worth fighting for, as are my children. The Gospel of Jesus Christ matters to me and I would die for it. After that, not much else will get my dander up. I'm not going to lose sleep because someone insulted my favorite sports team. I'm not going to be offended because someone holds a different political viewpoint than I do. And I'm not going to shatter because someone called me hurtful names. In the end, those things do not really matter. Instead, consider letting the *Teacup Syndrome* go!

Go get some.

7

VICTIMS AND VILLAINS

W hen I was doing postgraduate work, one of my professors did something that I had never experienced before. In a class on Scripture, which is my great love, the professor rejected one of my papers. This particular paper was an integral part of the requirements for fulfillment of the degree. In rejecting the chapter, she added,

"You have to go back and write it again because you didn't include any footnotes. You didn't cite any references or any sources." In other words, I quoted scripture because the chapter was about scripture, but the content of the argument was all my own personal thought. I didn't examine what other commentators said about the Scriptural passages I choose to cite. Every part of the paper was how I understood the particular passage I was exegeting. Frustrated, I replied in a annoyed tone,

"I followed your syllabus which didn't ask for any references to be included. You didn't ask us to cite anything. Your own syllabus actually sought our original thought."

"No," she replied, "this is a postgraduate degree. You have to cite sources."

So, I said to her (here's the snarky part), "You know, I recognize the need to cite sources while earning my master's degree, but in doctoral level work, I just figured you would want original thought." Ignoring my dig, the professor replied,

"No, no, we certainly want original thought, but we want to see your sources."

VICTIMS AND VILLAINS IN CONTEXT

Getting called out by another person is never a pleasant experience. To make ourselves feel better about the situation, we often devolve into something I call victim and villain behavior. By positioning ourselves as victims and the other person as a villain, we make it easier to justify our own behavior. Let's be totally honest, in the story above I was trying to pull a fast one on the professor. I mean, who in their right mind doesn't include references in a doctoral paper! But in order to justify my weak behavior, I told myself two clever stories. In the first story, I became the victim. How dare she do that to me? All I was trying to do was to produce original thought. I mean, this is a doctoral program for goodness sake. How could she do that to me? And in the blink of an eye, I became a victim. In the story I told myself, I was victimized by this particular person who had done something to me.

The second story I told myself exposed her villainy. How dare she? Who does she think she is? She's no real scholar with the pedigree to assault me and my work. She's just trying to make a name for herself and she's using me to gain an advantage in her career. And just like that, I made her out to be the villain. By telling myself these two stories, I relinquished any control I had over the situation. And it was all in order to let myself off the hook.

GOD'S INPUT

In the Orthodox Church's liturgical calendar, a story from the Gospel of Luke is read as the faithful draw closer to Great Lent. As we approach the celebration of the Lord's Crucifixion and Resurrection, the Church gets us warmed up by exploring a tale of victims and villains. In chapter 18, the Evangelist Luke imparts the story of the Pharisee and the Publican. Pharisees and Publicans were two well-known groups of people at the time of Jesus. Pharisees were the religious elite. They knew the Law backwards and forwards and were expected to be the most righteous of all of God's people. They exhibited leadership for the people and were held in high esteem. Publicans, on the other hand, were base and criminal people. They collected taxes and spent time with profligate people. As tax collectors, they collected money from their fellow Jews for the Roman government. The problem was, they often extorted a little extra to keep for themselves. Most people were not big fans of the Publicans.

In the story, these two men were in the temple praying. The Pharisee stood and offered this prayer, "God, I thank thee that I am not like other men, extortioners, unjust, adulterers, or even like this tax collector. I fast twice a week, I give tithes of all that I get," (Luke 18:11-12). The Pharisee was basically saying, "I'm such a good guy. I'm holy." The funny thing is, the Pharisees were supposed to be holy. That's what they were trained to be. Why should he claim any credit for what he was supposed to be doing? But by missing the true intent of holiness altogether, he made the Publican into a villain. "God, I thank you that I'm not like all the rest of these guys. In fact, God, do you know what I really thank you for? See this guy over here, this Publican? I'm especially thankful I'm not like him." Boom. The Pharisee is telling stories. His stories justify in his mind that he is the victim of unjust men and he positions someone else as the villain.

In contrast, righteousness was granted to the most unlikely of heroes. The Publican, who we know to have been a notoriously broken person, offered a pure and heartfelt prayer to God when, "the tax collector, standing far off, would not even lift up his eyes to heaven, but beat his breast, saying, 'God, be merciful to me a sinner!'" (Luke 18:13). There's no victim or villain story to be found. It was just simple recognition of his own sins and the request for forgiveness. The Publican took responsibility for his actions without making any excuses for why he did them. Curiously absent from his prayer was the mention of anyone else. Because of this, he was the one who left the temple in righteousness when Jesus said, "I tell you, this man went down to his house justified (made righteous) rather than the other; for every one who exalts himself will be humbled, but he who humbles himself will be exalted," (Luke 18:15).

℘ PRACTICAL POINTS

What action steps can we take to eliminate victimhood and villainy from our lives? We've got three practical points to help you. First, get comfortable with self-reflection. My partner and fellow Warrior Saint Greg has an excellent process that he follows when he feels the victim and villain stories creeping in. Before he responds to any criticism, he examines himself and replays the entirety of the events surrounding the situation in his mind. He doesn't just examine the other person's hurtful statement. Instead he goes all the way back to the beginning and replays his actions in his mind. It's kind of like Inigo Montoya waiting for Vizzini. Go back to the beginning and run the exchange again. Greg replays the events to see if any part of the other person's critique is legitimate. He won't allow himself to play the victim.

Here's where it gets tricky though. Fighting the urge to be right can be a challenging thing to do. To overcome the temptation to justify yourself, you must look at the story from two angles. What I mean is that every situation can be seen in at least two ways. The situation can be seen from your perspective or from the other person's perspective. Your job is to look at it from both perspectives. It's easy to run the version of the movie that justifies our behavior. What's harder—and crucifixional—is to play the version of the tape that fits the other person's narrative. If you do this honestly and fairly, you just might see things from a different perspective. It might be revealed to you that the criticisms are legitimate. Obviously, my professor was right and I was wrong no matter how badly I wanted it to be the other way around. I was only able to see that when I looked at it from her point of view. In the end, however, this was actually a great thing. In the end, that shift in mindset put me in a position of control and allowed me to make a positive change.

This leads us directly to practical point number two. In the story of the Publican and the Pharisee, Jesus brings the meaning home by saying that only those who humble themselves will be exalted (Luke 18:15). So, if exaltation is what you seek, then humble yourself, as painful as it may seem in the moment. You do that by always assuming you're wrong. I know, I know, that's nuts. No one can be wrong all the time. But by positioning yourself at the outset as being the instigator of the conflict, something dramatic happens. You gain control. The fundamental mistake of playing the role of victim and positing the other as the villain is that you have relinquished control to another person. By definition, victims are out of control. Things happen to them. Big bad villains do things to them. If that is true, then you have no choice but to accept whatever is done to you. God, however, is calling you to be a Warrior Saint and that means that you are exactly that: a warrior. Show me one warrior who sat back and allowed events to unfold with no say in the matter. I'm pretty sure you won't find one. And if you do, is that really the kind of warrior you want to imitate? My gut says you just shouted a resounding no. If you start with the assumption that you created the situation, then you also have control to repair it. But that kind of honest and humble introspection can only be done if you begin by assuming you were at fault.

Lastly, practical point number three is directly connected to the previous point. Let's assume that after an honest and humble self-reflection you discover that you were indeed innocent in the situation. The base, human reaction is to prove your innocence and tell the story that proves the other person is the villain. But do you always have to be right? Can you overlook some transgressions for the sake of harmony and peace in your relationships? We will explore this in greater detail in two forthcoming chapters, "Don't be Right. Win." and "Not Every Conversation", but for our purposes here, let the quick answer be yes, of course. In your lifetime, you will find that there are indeed some legitimate circumstances that are worth fighting for. Sometimes, we do need to stand up for ourselves and for truth. But those are rarely situations that involve our pride. Instead, the crucifixional approach is to allow a minor offense to go unaddressed so that we might foster peace and harmony in the world around us. Don't forget, healthy people do healthy things and broken people do broken things. By virtue of the fact that you are being unjustly accused shows that the person you are dealing with may be in the latter category. Those are the people Jesus has sent us to lead.

Go get some.

8

COURAGE

I had a junk pile on the side of the house. One of the things in that pile when we bought the home was a door leaning against the side of the house. It was an extra door to put in the home if it was ever needed. Over the years in the Arizona sun it dried and cracked. And whenever it rained the door got soggy and expanded. At some point it became unusable. One Saturday morning I said to myself, "You know what, just go clean that junk up. I can't stand the mess any more. Let's just get rid of all of it."

So, I went outside to clean up the junk pile. Being the biggest eyesore, I wanted to start with the door. When I began to lift the door off the side of the house, I heard it. It was as distinctive a sound as there could ever be. Right away I dropped the door. I didn't want to touch it. I knew what it was. Anyone who lives in Arizona and has seen a rattlesnake knows what that sound is. The sound of an angry diamondback can send chills down the bravest man's spine.

My first instinct was to run away but I was stuck. I couldn't leave it back there. My kids were playing outside! I had to figure it out. I inched the door back from leaning off the wall, bit by bit by bit, and sure enough, six feet of angry rattlesnake. She was just chilling in the shade and was mad that now someone was messing with her. The snake probably thought, "Why are you messing with me? I didn't do anything to anyone." At least not yet.

I thought, "Well, what am I going to do with it? I can't leave it there and I ain't touching it. No way, I'm not touching that thing." Something had to be done and I was frozen with fear.

We've all felt fear in our lives. Anyone who tells you they never experience fear is spinning yarn. Everyone gets afraid at one point or another. And you know what? That's perfectly okay. You're supposed to be afraid sometimes, because some things are truly scary! Fear is your body telling you, "Look out, there's danger ahead!" People who can't be honest enough to admit to their fears are only trying to protect their egos. And by now, we know that is not crucifixional living. Having fear can be normal and healthy and we need not be embarrassed about it.

So then what's the problem with fear? Why is it worthy of its own chapter? Fear gets its own chapter because if left unchecked, fear can lead us into one of the greatest opponents of crucifixional living: inaction. Fear can debilitate and lead us to just standing around, watching, doing nothing . . . inaction!

Courage, in contrast, is what we're after. Courage is not the absence of fear, courage is doing the right thing in spite of fear. Courage is not allowing fear to stop us from doing what we know to be right. And what we know to be right, especially as Warrior Saints, is to live a crucifixional life, to live a life where we sacrifice for other people in all things. Courage is my pool guy Travis recognizing, "I don't like the snake, but we've got to get it, and I'm going to act." But we'll get to that.

Fear comes in many faces, but the big three are:

1. The fear of what others will think;
2. The fear of failure;
3. The fear that it will be hard.

These three forms of fear often lead us to inaction—to do nothing when it's time to act. As we will see, having courage means conquering these fears by doing the right thing in spite of them. It means looking our fears right in the eyes, admitting that they exist and then kicking them right in the teeth.

₰ COURAGE IN CONTEXT

Thank the good Lord Jesus that Travis showed up. Travis is my pool guy. He's the best. By the way, if anybody needs a pool guy, I'm going to give a shout out to Travis. He's the best. Not just because of this story, but he's really good. So, Travis opened the back gate and said,

"Hey Fr. Chris, what are you doing?"

Pointing at the snake, all I could say was, "That."

Without blinking he said, "Oh, we'll just get it right now."

"What?" I shouted. I was afraid of it. I mean, literally I was afraid of it. It was a rattlesnake!

Travis responded, "Yeah, no problem." He had one of those long poles to scoop debris from the surface of the pool with, the kind with a net attached at the end. "It's simple," he said, taking the net and pinning the snake's head against the side of the house. Now the snake was really going nuts. "Just grab it with these pliers and we'll kill it."

Wait, what? Seriously, what was he thinking? "I ain't touching that thing. No way," I said. Because I'm a giver and love other people so much, I want them to have opportunity to grow. I said, "Travis, tell you what. I don't want to take this opportunity away from you. I'll hold the pole and you can grab it." He just sagged his head in shame as if to say, "You're such a pansy." He relinquished the pole, grabbed the pliers and pinched the snake's head so it couldn't bite him.

As he was holding it and it was flipping all around, he told me, "Now go get your hedge clippers and cut its head off." Seriously, this dude has issues. I didn't really want to kill it because in spite of its dreadfulness it was a beautiful animal. It was fierce and as deadly as a predator could potentially be, but it had to be done. We cut its head off and ended the drama. There's even Facebook pictures of the incident.

Throughout the whole ordeal something fascinating happened. I was afraid. I didn't have the courage to deal with it and yet Travis had no problem. He just acted.

I said to Travis, "Aren't you afraid of that stuff? I mean, you're working in backyards every day, so you probably see that kind of stuff all the time." And then he humbled me. Knocked the wind right out of my sails. He said,

"Of course, I'm afraid of it, but you've got to deal with problems, so I dealt with it." Floored, all I could muster was,

"Oh." He had courage and I didn't.

♪ GOD'S INPUT

The great news is that God offers us comfort in the face of our fears. The Prophet Isaiah says, "For I, the Lord your God, hold your right hand; it is I who say to you, 'Fear not, I will help you,'" (Is. 41:13). This is awesome confirmation that we are not alone as we face our fears and challenges in life. God is with us holding our right hand. Let's be clear about that part. I don't think "God holding our right hand" is referring to a literal holding of our hand as if we were walking together on a beach with the proverbial two sets of footprints that become one when God does the work for us. God doesn't do our work for us. He is not a magician sitting on a big chair in the puffy white clouds waving a magic wand and making everything all right. That's not the God I find in Scripture.

By holding our right hand, Isaiah is telling us to trust in God and to trust in His Way. God is telling us that if we listen to His words and live the Way He's asking us to live, we will conquer the monster of fear. What is that Way? By now, you already know what I'm going to say: crucifixional living. The willingness to sacrifice our comforts, desires, needs—even our self—in order to win, that's crucifixional living. God is reassuring us that if we trust His Way and follow it, it works. Sure, it'll be difficult. But it's supposed to be. And you want it to be. Becoming a Warrior Saint means exactly that: you have to become a warrior. And warriors battle with their enemies, often earning scars and wounds. But it's the only way to win. Standing on the sidelines will cost you every time.

PRACTICAL POINTS

Our practical point for dealing with the three big fears above is pretty simple: shift your mindset. That's it. It really is that simple. Shift your mindset. Conventional wisdom and even fear itself tells us that we should worry about what others think, that we should avoid failure at all costs and that we should seek only to do easy tasks. What could be further from the truth? This practical point is that you must flip those thoughts upside down and shift your mindset. Make sure you have some haters, fail as much as possible and do the hardest things you possibly can.

First, the fear of what others will think is a major culprit in our inaction. We allow others' impressions to guide so much of what we do in our lives. Some have even called this need approval addiction. For some reason it's important that people like us, approve of us, validate us. That's probably built into each of us as relational beings. To conquer this need first requires a shift in mindset where you not only seek to be comfortable with critics, but where you actively seek critics. Yep. You read that right. Find more critics. I love how Grant Cardone says it, "Baby, if you have five haters, you need to go get you five more!" He's totally correct in this regard. Having haters can be a good thing in so many ways. The first way is that it witnesses to the fact that you're in action. Haters reveal that you're doing something, moving, acting. People rarely, if ever, criticize someone for doing nothing. Sure, they may call you a lazy bum, but they're actually happier with you sitting on the sidelines because it means you're not competition. If you get up, start taking action and producing, you then become competition to them. And their criticism is a witness to that fact.

To be fair, their criticism may be correct. We should always be humble enough to ask ourselves the tough questions so that we can improve. But more often than not, haters attack you and your work because they are ashamed of themselves. They're ashamed because they're sitting on the sidelines watching you do what they know they should be doing. They're jealous because they know in their hearts, they should be doing the very thing you're doing. They should be trying to better themselves. Haters attack others who make them uncomfortable because they know they themselves are inactive. Rather than say good for you when you're in action, they attempt to make themselves feel better by criticizing you. It's usually a cover up for their own fears and insecurities. Remember, if you have some haters, go get some more. It means you're on to something!

The second shift in mindset is in regard to failure. We're so often afraid to attempt what we've been called to do because we don't want to mess it up. We don't want to fail. Think about it. From the very beginning of our rational existence we're constantly taught that failure will produce bad results. If you don't stop climbing that tree, you're going to fall and get hurt. If you don't get all A's, you won't get into Harvard. If you invest in a risky venture you could lose your money. You can't create a marketing campaign on your own. If you don't spend money on advertising, you'll never sell your product. She'll never go out on a date with you. You're writing a book? You'll be the laughing stock of the publishing world! And on and on and on. Perhaps more than any other fear, the fear of failure has left more people clinging to the sidelines of inaction.

The shift in mindset that Warrior Saints are looking for is quite different. We're actually hoping to go out there and fail. That's right, we're looking for failure. Of course, no one wants to fail *in the end*. But no one gets to the end unscathed. Every journey has potholes, speed bumps and curves in the road. That doesn't mean you don't drive your car does it? You have to make an effort. You have to try. Sure, you're going to fail sometimes, and in that failure comes the greatest learning and the greatest movement forward. Thomas Edison failed with the lightbulb over and over again. Michael Jordan lost in the playoffs to the Celtics and Pistons repeatedly. The Apostle Peter renounced Jesus three times before the Crucifixion. But these men didn't hide from failure, they used their failures as springboards to their successes. Edison gave us light, Jordan won six championships and St. Peter became the rock upon which God built His Church. Shift your mindset to seek failure, for through it is the best way to success.

Finally, let's look at the concept of hard with a totally different mindset. Remember, the world wants us to find the easy way. But we actually prefer hard. It's more fun and brings greater rewards. Sure, the rewards come at the end of the hard work. But it's actually gratifying, unlike the pseudo wins we get for taking the easy road and popping the magic pill. I really do believe we actually like hard work, that we are built for it and prefer it. But we have been brainwashed into thinking that hard is bad. All of the advertising and marketing we're bombarded with is attempting to sell us easy. And we don't really think about it; we just agree and go along on our merry way. But we're more miserable because of it. We actually want the hard work and the suffering and the pain. It's way more fun!

My bride is the best thing that has happened to me in my life. But at the beginning she made me work for it. It took everything I could think of to convince her to go out with me on a first date. Even though we both had a blast, there was nothing I could do to get her to go out on a second date with me. Knowing that I wanted to become an Orthodox priest was not how she envisioned her future husband. And so, she told me no. And no again. And again. It was certainly the hardest failure I've ever had to face. But I didn't quit and I kept learning how to be the man she needed me to be, priest or not. And eventually she agreed to another date. The rest, as they say, is history. We've been married for over twenty years and are blessed with the healthiest relationship I could have ever asked for. And the joy I felt when she finally agreed to go out on that second date was worth all the pain and the suffering along the way.

As we examine our own lives, our own suffering and our own fears, it's time to reflect and say, "All right. It's okay that I'm afraid. I have fear, but I'm still going to act because I have courage."

Go get some.

9

ALWAYS DO THE RIGHT THING

Have you ever worried about what other people thought of you? Have you felt rejected or of little value when someone criticized you personally or something that you did? You are certainly not alone if you have. The desire to be accepted and affirmed by other people is something intrinsic to all of us. We need to be accepted by others. No man is an island, as they say. In the Ancient Near East, for example, at the time of King David, to be rejected by the community was a death sentence. It was virtually impossible to live alone outside of the safety and commerce of the community.

There's a lot of discussion in our world today whether or not to care about what other people think of us. Many take the position that you shouldn't be concerned with how others see you. Be who you are, express yourself and don't worry if you are made fun of or if others mock you. Don't worry if they look at you and think of you as odd or funny. "You do you." There is certainly a modicum of truth and merit in that position. It is healthy to be free to express yourself exactly as you are. In fact, in the previous chapter, "Courage", we explored some practical ways to overcome what some call approval addiction.

⸫ THE RIGHT THING IN CONTEXT

I prefer the other position. You should care what others think of you, but with a caveat which we'll learn shortly. I've worked very hard during the twenty-two years of my ministry to ensure that my name and my reputation are highly regarded. I want other people to know that I'm a good man. I want other people to know that I spend my whole life serving other people. I want a good reputation. There is no sin in that. I work very hard to make sure that my words and my actions are in alignment with the Gospel of Jesus Christ so that everything I do is appropriate and upholding of my reputation. My name matters to me.

The temptation that we face when caring about what others think, however, is to become people pleasers. "I feel good if you feel good." Or we choose noncontroversial and nonconfrontational responses in order to avoid any backlash. "Let's talk about mundane things so we don't have to fight." The desire to preserve our name and to be looked upon with high regard often tempts us with inaction, or worse, to do the wrong thing so that nobody talks badly about us. The caveat we referred to above is to care about what others think but always do the right thing. Always protect and preserve your name but not at the expense of doing the right thing. In all things, Warrior Saints must take the right action.

⸫ GOD'S INPUT

There is a tragic story in 2 Samuel chapter 11 about King David. During a time of heavy fighting with the Ammonites, a neighboring tribe of Jerusalem, the armies of the king were sent to a town named Rabbah for war. The king, however, stayed home in the capital city while all of his fighting men went off to battle. One day while he was walking on his rooftop, he saw a beautiful woman named Bathsheba. She was so striking and so lovely that his passion was enflamed and he wanted to make love to her. Being the king, he called her into the castle and had sex with her. Aside from the fact that David abused his power and manipulated this woman into a sexual encounter, she happened to be the wife of his close friend, Uriah the Hittite. To complicate matters even further, as a result of that encounter, Bathsheba became pregnant with the king's illegitimate child.

Just when you think the story couldn't get any more tragic, David stooped to new lows in order to preserve his name. David's problem was that her husband Uriah was away at war and would know that the child wasn't his. So rather than just come clean and say, "Look, Uriah my buddy, I'm sorry, I had an affair with your wife," David did something drastic. Ignoring his responsibility for the sin and caring more for how others perceived and spoke of him, David committed a sin even more evil than the initial tryst. He sent his friend Uriah to the frontlines of the battle in the hopes that he would be killed. And sure enough, Uriah was killed. King David was more interested in avoiding shame for his sinful actions than taking personal responsibility. As a result, he had his friend put to death. These tragic events would ultimately lead to David's shame, causing him to live the remainder of his life in repentance. The crowning product of his shame and repentance is the penitential Psalm 51 (50).

I've said before and will say again that you should protect and preserve your good name but not at the expense of right action. Warrior Saints are always ready to do the right thing even when that means others will speak ill of us. I can tell you that in my more than two decades of priesthood, I have often made decisions that others don't quite understand. How could they without knowing all the details. And yet I made those decisions because they were the right decisions to make. I have often received backlash or heard gossip about what a poor decision I made. In some cases, I could anticipate that happening before I even put the decision into play. When confronting difficult choices, the temptation is to take the easy road because you may think that if you do the right thing they're going to talk about you. I've had to force myself as often as possible to make sure I do the right thing anyway. Even when that means my name takes a hit.

To be crucifixional and live as Warrior Saints means confronting the possibility that we might very well be talked about for taking a particular action. If it's right, take it anyway. We must always do the right thing no matter what. Better to have your good name briefly besmirched for right action than to pretend to be something you're not. As Warrior Saints, we recognize it will be difficult to face the backlash and gossip, but that is what we're all about. That's exactly what we're here to do. We're here to find the difficult things—the truth—and do it. It is our responsibility to preserve our name, but more importantly to always do the right thing no matter the consequences.

⸹ PRACTICAL POINTS

In order to do the right thing in every situation, we must first make sure our decisions are always well thought out. Rash decisions are almost always bad decisions. There is a myriad of different ways to think through the decisions we're called to make. My brother-in-law Waleed is a thoughtful and intelligent man. I admire him greatly because he thinks before he speaks. Very rarely do you hear him say something that he hasn't already thought through. I'm quite different, I speak to think. I like to practice my conversations and decisions out loud. My brain works through ideas during the process of speaking out loud. So, I either have to talk through the situation with another person (pray for my team who endures most of this!) or simply out loud by myself in the car. (Yes, I'm that weird dude talking to himself on the freeway!) Through this process, I'm able to run through all of the scenarios and the consequences for the decision I'm about to make. For example, I've been seen driving my car around in circles saying, "Okay, Fr. Chris, if you do a then b will happen. If you do x then y will happen." As I talk through it, I am able to process and decide what would be the right decision. You may be like me and need to speak with another person to bounce the idea around with you. Or, you may be like my brother-in-law and simply need to spend time in quiet reflection to think through the scenario. Either route you choose, your first practical point is to think about what you're doing and avoid making rash decisions, especially the big ones. To do this, you need a buffer.

The second practical point in this chapter is about creating a buffer. This point is so important that we'll address it again and again throughout this book. At this point, let's at least understand that bad timing is one of the greatest deterrents to doing the right thing. We encounter people throughout the day, many of whom make requests and demands on our time. It is not uncommon to feel compelled to make an on-the-spot decision. To be sure, some decisions can be made immediately. However, if we're not careful, as these requests pile up, we can find ourselves overwhelmed with a packed and ineffective schedule.

Most decisions should be made after careful consideration. So, we must politely say to the other person, "I'm not going to decide at this moment. I'm not going to decide until I've thought it through." How do we do this? We do it by creating a buffer. One of the habits that we must develop is the ability to say, "Thank you. Let me get back to you." I know we feel compelled to respond immediately because somebody asks for our time. But most often, it is to our advantage and to the advantage of the people we are serving to thoroughly think through the commitment we want to make. It is not inappropriate to say, "Let me get back to you shortly." I have a little trick that I do now on Sundays after church. When all of my people are present, many of them approach me asking to schedule appointments with them on the spot. Because I love them, my temptation is to comply and pull out my calendar and commit right then and there. But I've learned that by doing so I make a lot of bad decisions. Instead, I have implemented a buffer. At this point in my tenure, I ask them to reach out to my assistant, who does all of my scheduling, and she can get us together. In this, I have created the buffer that I'm looking for and I'm not making rash decisions on the spot.

Our final practical point is to be committed to stand alone. Know going in that right action is hard action. Very often, doing the right thing is the least popular decision. We've already discussed that gossip and backlash from the mob is hiding around the very next corner. Having to stand up for what you believe in is hard and most normal people shy away from that responsibility. But we're not trying to be normal men and women. We're becoming Warrior Saints. We're becoming exceptional human beings who insist upon the truth always prevailing. Sure, there will be mobs who will try to cancel you, but remember, no real change ever happened in this world without great struggle. There are countless heroes who have stood their ground, even when they stood alone. Dr. Martin Luther King, Jr., Mother Theresa and Abraham Lincoln come to mind. They spoke the truth even when it was not popular to do so. More important are the heroes of old who inspire us in the Christian faith. Think of the prophets Samuel and Elijah who stood up to kings and mobs. John the Baptist who lost his head for speaking the truth. The Apostle Paul who led a tumultuous life of beatings, imprisonment and ultimately beheading for preaching the Gospel unabashedly. Of course, the greatest of all, the Lord Jesus who died alone on the Cross to save mankind. He died not just for speaking the truth but for being The Truth. Yeah, it's hard but it's right. You're not reading this book because you want an easy life. You're reading this book because you want to be the very best you can be. To do that means that sometimes we will have to stand alone. It will take courage, but be of good cheer! Be the lion and become a Warrior Saint.

Go get some.

10

CHASING THE QUIET

I was having a particularly rough day. Everything was annoying. My mind was just not capable of handling everything that was being thrown at me. I was frustrated and stressed out. I just wasn't behaving like a very nice person. Needing to find a quick break from the chaos, I tried driving endlessly around town. My hopes were that some solitude in my car would give me a much-needed buffer. At one point, I stopped at a gas station to fill up the car with gas. I deliberately left my cell phone in the car. A seemingly peculiar place, I thought I was going to find two minutes of peace and quiet at the gas station. But then a funny thing happened. I pulled my credit card out of the machine and placed the nozzle in the gas tank. Before I could click the handle, a woman started shouting at me asking me if I wanted to buy something. Turning around there was no one to be found. There was, however, a TV screen on the pump. And an advertisement was playing in which the shouting woman was again asking me to buy something. I couldn't do anything but laugh. I thought to myself, is there nowhere in this world to find quiet?

⸙ CHASING THE QUIET IN CONTEXT

There is a lot of noise in our world. It is so hard for us as men and women in today's hyper-connected world to find quiet. And I don't mean the kind of quiet that you find when you go to a movie theater. I mean quiet in our minds and the ability to find rest and peace in the depths of our soul. There are constant reminders, notifications and alarms that vie for our attention. We have appointments to keep, phone calls to make, texts to return and of course, the myriad of Facebook, Instagram, Twitter and Snapchat notifications from our friends and family.

Emails constantly blow up our inbox. People are constantly vying for our time and asking that we give them those few precious moments we have in the day to use for a little quiet and reflection. And that's not to mention the constant bombardment of noise that we find filling our screens, TV, YouTube and movie theaters. Even in restaurants, TV screens are hung all around the walls. Everywhere we go there is noise. Unfortunately, I don't think that the noise is a good thing. I'm an avid tech fan and definitely see the benefits and the beauties of the technological advances of our modern age. I use them all as much as possible, but also remain cognizant that the constant barrage of noise is by design. I believe that the corporate monsters who run the world use noise to keep us busy and distracted. When we're distracted by the noise, the more we purchase, the less we think and the harder it becomes to see the truth. If we don't control the noise, we can easily become automata. To quote Rage Against the Machine, "They say jump and we say how high."

§ GOD'S INPUT

To overcome the noise, we have to chase the quiet. There are mountains and mountains of data that tell us how essential a clear mind is to good health, both physical and emotional. This does not even take into account the ability to be a productive member of the human race. It's impossible for us to make our highest contribution to anyone or anything if we're always sluggish and our minds are swimming inside our heads. More than that, it is virtually impossible to find spiritual health if you are lost in the chaos of noise.

In Psalm 46, we hear a passionate verse, often quoted by people who are on their faith journey seeking closeness to God. Though these mentions are well-meaning, the rich depths of what the Psalmist is trying to say are often overlooked. The verse says, "Be still and know that I am God," (Ps. 46:10). Some translations use the words, "Be quiet and know that I am God." I think that has a lot to do with keeping your mouth shut. Literally! If we are always talking, then we are never listening.

There is an interesting phenomenon within the artistic tradition of the Orthodox Church. Iconography holds a place of prominence in the churches and homes of Orthodox faithful. Images of the Lord, of His mother and of His saints adorn the walls of every Orthodox dwelling. A careful examination of these icons reveals something quite peculiar. In all of the icons, the human figures have really big ears and mouths that are shut. The exaggeration cannot be missed. This is not done because people of bygone ages had abnormally large ears and didn't know how to talk. It's because the iconographer is trying to impart to us that if we want to hear the Word of God, we have to stop talking and listen. That cannot be done if our lips are always moving!

In our hyper-connected world, there's a lot of noise that we may be tempted to respond to. If we constantly allow the noise to dominate our hearts and minds, we'll quickly find that there is never really any time to stop and listen and to hear what God is saying. We must be quiet and know that He is God. We must find some space where our mind can actually be empty and where we can really—even if only for a few brief moments—turn off the noise. I know that we all understand how essential this is, but it is an incredibly hard thing to do. On that fateful day at the gas station I found it nearly impossible. To chase the quiet means to actively seek that moment of physical quiet and also, more importantly, to find quiet for your mind.

℘ PRACTICAL POINTS

So how do we chase quiet so that we can know that God is God? First, we have to find time for prayer or meditation. To be honest, even that's not really the answer. Time isn't lost "out there" where we somehow need to find and rescue it. Our time is precisely that, *our* time. We actually have to *make* time. You are in control of your time and your schedule. As you will see in other chapters on time, no one will give us time for free. No one will magically free up space in our calendar. In fact, you're probably well aware that others actually try to take our time from us. Instead, we have to consciously plan time for quiet and prayer. Time for prayer and quiet is something you must schedule by design. Simply put, you must write in your calendar—every single day of your life—an actual appointment of five minutes or ten minutes or a half an hour for quiet meditation and prayer. Be deliberate about planning time for meditation or it will never happen. I once heard someone say that you schedule what matters to you. If you want to chase the quiet, put it in your calendar.

Our second practical point is to find a repetitive prayer or meditation. It can be so wonderful and beautiful to speak freely to your Maker from your heart. Those moments are to be treasured and should never be forsaken. But there is something beautiful about a structured and repetitive prayer. If you're like me, you'll notice that after a certain amount of time you begin to memorize your prayers, and in that memorization, you are able to really concentrate and focus on the words and what they mean. At some point the prayer begins to happen all by itself and your focus can be on the emptiness of the quiet. I promise you God will fill it.

Though we should never stop saying prayers that come directly from the heart, we cannot neglect to build a prayer discipline. A prayer discipline is designing a specific set of prayers you will say each and every day in the same order and in the same physical place. People like discipline, even if we claim not to, and our most significant work is done through repetition. If you are unsure of what to pray, seek a spiritual guide or a father confessor—or even call me—to help you establish a rule of prayer that you can follow each day.

Our last practical point, and this is perhaps the biggest challenge of the modern era, you must break free from the chains of your screens. There have to be moments—absolutely must be moments—where you don't look at the phone or the tablet or the TV or the computer or the laptop. Being tethered to those devices is to openly invite all the noise of the world to bombard you. Chase the quiet and trust that when you find it, your mind will be clearer and sharper. Then you can make your requests known to God and he will hear them. Then, and only then, in that still, quiet voice, you will know God as God.

We end this chapter with a beautiful verse from St. Paul's Epistle to the Philippians. "Do not be anxious about anything, but in everything by prayer and supplication with thanksgiving, let your requests be known to God. And the peace of God, which surpasses all understanding will guard your hearts and your minds in Christ Jesus," (Phil. 4:6-7). Such beautiful words. I hope you take them to heart chasing the quiet.

Go get some.

PART 2

MANKIND IN RELATION TO OTHERS

11

SERVE

My mother is one of the most selfless people I know. The entirety of her life has been about serving others, most notably my sister and me. She was made a widow at a very young age when my father was killed by a drunk driver. At the time, my sister and I were six and seven years old, respectively. She could have chosen any number of directions to focus her life on after the accident happened. It would have been completely understandable—maybe even expected—that after her grief and healing, she turned her attentions on her own well-being. While no one would have blamed her for seeking her own happiness, that is not what she decided to do. Instead, she dedicated her life to the service of her children, raising us to become the best people we could be. She certainly succeeded with my sister. Clearly, I am biased, but my sister is very much like my mother and one of the finest people I know. I am constantly inspired by her. I, on the other hand, am a far cry from either of them, but any good in me is because my mother has served me throughout my life.

Serving another person often has negative connotations in our culture today. For some, it even conjures up images of slavery and oppression to those who don't know how to look at it. But to serve is not about your position in life. To serve is about an attitude you take on. It is an attitude of putting other people ahead of yourself. The attitude of serving others before self is the essence of crucifixional living. To serve requires that we look first to the needs of another before we look to the needs of ourself. In a world that seems to only focus on becoming the big shot at the table, this may seem counterintuitive. In his book, *Leadership Lessons of Jesus*, Bob Briner shows us how wrong that worldview is when he says, "Find the servant, and you've found your leader. He's not the big shot sitting at the head of the table. He's the one out in the kitchen serving the meal." And to serve another person means there is a great deal of sacrifice involved. It means we have to be crucifixional.

§ SERVICE IN CONTEXT

My mother could have easily been selfish after my father's untimely death. She was beautiful and still young and any number of suitors would have gladly made a life with her. Some even tried. But she was willing to sacrifice that life so that she could dedicate herself to raising my sister and me. Along with raising two children, she spent the first few years after my father's death in public service battling the legal system to raise the drinking age from eighteen to twenty-one in the state of West Virginia where we lived and where my dad's car crash took place. And though we were blessed to live comfortably, she sacrificed a lot of her needs and desires to make sure that as a family, we had enough money to live without having to work a 9-5 job. She sacrificed a love life and her material desires to make certain her children were solid. And she sacrificed her effort and spare time to ensure no underage West Virginian could drink alcohol and take another life behind the wheel. Through her efforts, in 1986 the age limit for drinking alcohol in West Virginia was finally raised to twenty-one.

It's not surprising that she immediately leapt into a life of service after my father's death. She was raised by parents who taught her to serve others because they themselves were servants. In WWII, my maternal grandfather served in the U.S. Army Medical Corps. In early 1943, he was stationed in Guadalcanal. At one point during intense enemy resistance, a sniper had pinned down a group of soldiers from an elevated position. Many U.S. soldiers had been shot and were dying. If they were not given medical attention immediately, some of those brave men would have certainly died. My grandfather, the doctor in the Medical Corps, crawled with his medical bag back and forth across enemy lines to tend to fallen soldiers. When he shared his experience of that day with us, he told of a soldier who was badly wounded and needed an IV while still across the enemy line. Whenever he tried to raise his arm to elevate the IV bag, the sniper would shoot at him. His heroic actions saved that man's life. The most striking part of the story was noting that at no point in his telling did he mention any fear of losing his own life. His only concern was helping the wounded soldier. His selflessness that day earned him the Silver Star Medal.

Forgive me if I come across as boastful about my family. I am merely humbled by their courage and selfless sacrifice and proud to come after them. With such clarity they so exhibited what service to others means that I could not help but be inspired to a live of service myself. From a very young age, I was taught that to serve means to put another person in front of you. That is crucifixional living.

In contrast, the modern world is very much self-centered. From our youth, we're taught to "get mine" and to "look out for number one." Putting the needs of another person ahead of your own is strangely out of context in 21st century North America. Burger King's slogan is "Have it Your Way". L'Oreal wants you to buy their make-up "Because You're Worth It". Apple has even named their products to cater to your ego with iPhone, iPad, iPod and iMac.

As Warrior Saints, however, we're looking for something much different. To serve another person you must start from the premise that you are second. We are called to put the other person first. To do so, is to follow Jesus and live a crucifixional life.

§ GOD'S INPUT

Putting aside the self in order to serve another human being is the focus of this book. But it is nowhere more clearly defined than in chapter 10 of the Gospel of Mark. Beginning in verse 32, Jesus tells His disciples that He is going up to Jerusalem to face mocking, spitting, scourging and ultimately death for the sake and salvation of mankind. This message is the foundation of what it means to be crucifixional. He then confirms that after three days, He will rise from the dead, proving the salvific nature of His Cross. But then something funny happens. James and John, two of His main disciples ask Him to do something for them. When questioned what that might be, they reply, "Grant us to sit, one at Your right hand and one at Your left, in Your glory," (v. 37). This is just stunning! Immediately after He tells them that His road leads to the Cross, where He will voluntarily allow Himself to be sacrificed in order to serve mankind, they ask to be put in glory. It's as if they're asking to be the big shots at the head of the table. James and John are certainly saints of the Church and I don't mean to disparage them, but in this instance, they reveal the worldview of putting the self first. Their interest wasn't in serving others or following Jesus as He made the ultimate sacrifice to serve the world. They were only concerned with getting theirs. In the passage that follows, Jesus exposes the world's position on greatness and then contrasts it with crucifixional living, saying that to be great is to serve:

> "You know that those who are supposed to rule over the Gentiles lord it over them, and their great men exercise authority over them. But it shall not be so among you; but whoever would be great among you must be your servant, and whoever would be first among you must be slave of all. For the Son of Man also came not to be served but to serve, and to give His life as a ransom for many," (vv. 42-45).

The great men who are to lord over the Gentiles throw their authority around and expect to be treated like kings. They want to be the big shots at the head of the table. They want to be served. But for those who want to follow Christ, it shall not be so. Instead, followers of Christ—Warrior Saints who want to live a crucifixional life—are to serve others. Greatness comes from serving other. Using the parlance of the times, Jesus uses the words "servant" (*diakonos*) and "slave" (*doulos*) to reorient our mindset towards service. You want to be great? Then you must first serve. And the model of that for us is the Lord himself. He didn't come to be the big shot at the head of the table, though indeed, in the history of the world He is the only one who should have been the big shot. But He came to serve and give His life for all mankind. That's the type of crucifixional living. We have been called to be the antitype and follow Him.

So how do we do that? How can we implement crucifixional living into our daily lives and put others first in order to serve them? Like we said earlier, it's all about your attitude. You can constantly try to put yourself first and "get yours" if you like. But a quick glance around will expose the error of that line of thinking. Instead, we must be intentional with our attitude and wake up each and every morning with the plan to serve at least one person that day.

⸙ PRACTICAL POINTS

Our first practical point is to start with the small things. Our natural inclination is to race out of the gates and arrive at the finish line quickly. But that's not how life actually works. We want to make an impact equivalent to Mother Theresa before 9:00 a.m. A noble desire to be sure, but when we don't accomplish that on day one, it's easy to become discouraged. That discouragement can lead to frustration, or worse, quitting. But what if you started super small? What if you began with quick little wins and built up some momentum? Would that not help solidify this new attitude? You bet it would. Maybe start by doing someone else's chores for them in the house. Is it your spouse's responsibility to take out the trash? Maybe you could do it for them first thing in the morning. Perhaps your colleague at work has a pressing project and you know she's been working late into the night and starting again early in the morning. Could you surprise her with a cup of coffee when you arrive at the office? Or your son has a baseball game this Thursday and he needs to practice his fastball? What if you played catch for thirty minutes after homework is done? Though these examples may seem trite, they all set in motion the attitude of doing something for someone else. And that's super important because to own an attitude of serving others costs more than a one-time payment. It is an ongoing investment you have to make. The Roman Catholic saint, Therese de Lisieux is credited with saying, "Miss no opportunity of making some small sacrifice, here by a smiling look, there by a kindly word; always doing the smallest right and doing it all for love". Start small and let the momentum build.

Our second practical point is to spend time with the poor and less fortunate. It can be a beautiful blessing to give money to the homeless man standing on the street corner. It can also be misleading. By doing so, we can hopefully help a hungry man eat, but it is also easy and comfortable. In this way, I can avoid the discomfort of interacting with another human being. I can simply stick my money out of the car window and give that homeless guy some cash. When I do that, however, a lot of things can go wrong. First, I have dehumanized the person. He's not John or Ron or Bill, he's "that homeless guy." Second, I have not challenged myself to do anything really uncomfortable. I've only made an attempt to make myself feel better in a comfortable way. That feeling is hollow, at best. Instead, spend some time—I mean real time—serving other human beings. Make it a regular occurrence to volunteer in a soup kitchen or orphanage. Mentor a young person at your local Boys and Girls Club. Every church I know has some type of outreach ministry, so get involved. By doing so, you are now spending time with actual people, not just "that homeless guy." When you do, you will discover something incredible and unexpected. These people actually do more for you than you do for them. They will soften your heart. I know it's not easy to soften our heart to the poor at first, but keep at it and you will find it gets easier and easier. In *The 21 Indispensable Qualities of a Leader*, John C. Maxwell eloquates this so wonderfully. "Begin serving with your body, and your heart will eventually catch up."[8] I absolutely love this! The best way to overcome our discomfort

---

[8] Page 39.

with serving others is to just start physically. In time, as you listen and talk with "that homeless guy" you will quickly see that he is a human being no different than you. He even has a name.

Finally, sacrifice something of yours to serve another person. That could be your finances, but maybe even more importantly, it could be your time. Two feelings that people so desperately need today are affirmation and value. Our political movements have burdened us so heavily with conforming to certain identities that we cease to matter as individuals. We are only valuable if we are part of some larger whole, another piece of the machine. But this simply isn't true. Each person is made in God's image and thus extremely valuable. So often we lose the belief in that truth. That is not a problem reserved for the homeless and poor, though they certainly experience it, but also for our children, parents, spouses, friends and co-workers. All of us at some point face the fear that we don't matter or that we're of little or no value. Nothing could be further from the truth. By spending time—our most precious commodity—with another human being, we show that person we think they are of value. Talk with people, listen to people and let them know you love them. You cannot do any of those things without spending a little bit of quality time.

Our life as a Warrior Saint is a life of service. That means that we must sacrifice a little bit of our self for the sake and well-being of another. This is crucifixional living at its finest.

Go get some.

12

LISTEN

Fellas, I know you'll understand what I'm talking about. Something happened that should never have happened. You probably won't believe me, but I'm telling the truth. It happened. About a year ago, my bride Ally and I were driving to meet some friends for dinner and we got into an argument. The argument started because I told her that on this particular Sunday night, we had dinner plans at 7:00 P.M. with some friends, but she didn't remember. She replied,

"You didn't tell me."

I said, "I told you."

"You didn't tell me."

"I told you."

"You didn't tell me."

And on it went. The argument was focused on whether I told her about the dinner plans or not. I often tease my sweet bride about her split personality. "My other wife heard it."

She said, "No, there's no such thing, and you didn't tell me."

As we got close to the restaurant, I finally said in a firm tone, "Babe, I told you!" Then she said these words to me, words I will never forget for as long as I live,

"Well, those may be the words you said, but that's not what I heard."

Time slowed. Somewhere in the distance the Mormon Tabernacle

Choir began singing Handel's Hallelujah chorus. The clouds parted and a beautiful beam of sunlight burst through the windshield of the car. A calm wind blew through the car windows and my bride's hair was wafting ever so lovely in the breeze. No lie, Kenny Loggins music was playing in the background. It was glorious. I looked at her and I said,

"Did you just do that?" Of course, she gave me the look. I asked politely, "Did you just admit to me the words that every man knows and wants to hear but yet never gets to hear? Am I the only guy in the history of marriage to hear that you actually don't listen to what I say and just do whatever you feel like?" *That look again.* Needless to say, dinner that night was not the most pleasant meal I've ever had.

A few days before this dinner, I had gotten sick and was taking a cycle of antibiotics. This is important because as we pulled into the parking lot I said, "Babe, let's have a cocktail to celebrate and to thank our friends."

She replied, "Look, you're taking antibiotics and the doctor told you not to drink alcohol and take antibiotics at the same time or you'll get sick."

I said, "It'll be fine. I'll only have one drink. I just want to celebrate with them."

So, we ordered cocktails, bourbon being my poison of choice, and the night was off to a fabulous start (minus: *the look*). About that time, the waitress appeared and told us the dinner specials for the evening. "We have oysters on the half shell tonight," she told us. I love oysters on the half shell. Nice Blue Points. Blue Points may not be the best oysters in the world, but for Arizona, they're great. Oyster after oyster after oyster, I threw them down as fast as they could bring them. Ally looked at me and said,

"You're going to be sick."

I said, "Babe, I'll be fine. But if not, you'll help me, won't you? Surely, you'll help me. If my stomach does get upset, you'll help me." *That look again.*

So, as we ate oyster after oyster, the company and the meal were perfect. Until about three quarters of the way through, at which point I started to get hot and sweaty. My vision went blurry and I knew that my stomach was not my friend that night. It's like that moment when you hope everything will be all right but you know, in the end, everything will not be all right. As my vision worsened, I had to give Ally the keys to drive us home. With an almost playful gleefulness she said,

"I told you that bourbon, oysters and antibiotics don't mix." She found it funny that all the way home I was writhing in pain. I didn't want to talk. I couldn't talk because I was afraid. I was very afraid. By the time we got home, the race was on. I sprinted into the bathroom and spent the next few minutes by myself emptying the entire contents of my stomach. After fifteen minutes of agony from mixing bourbon, oysters and antibiotics, she came into the bathroom. Standing over me as I was writhing in pain, she looked at me and said, "Are you okay?" I looked at her in exasperation and in agony. I said,

"Babe, help me. You said you would help me." And with cold, steely eyes, she looked at me and said,

"Well, those may be the words you said, but that's not what I heard." And she walked out of the bathroom.

⸎ LISTEN IN CONTEXT

Clearly bourbon, oysters and antibiotics don't mix well. But a larger problem was at play here which was my inability to sincerely listen to another person and allow them to communicate with me. I should have allowed Ally to share her thoughts fully with me in order to process them before responding. I am the absolute worst at this. When in conversation with someone, I'm often guilty of one of the many flaws of poor communication. The first of which is that I speak to think. Smarter men than I think before they speak. That's not me. I speak to think. So, when I'm talking, I'm actually working my thoughts out. Out loud. God bless my bride, children and staff for having to endure this painful exercise. This causes me to commandeer just about every conversation as I work through my challenges out loud.

Second, when in a conversation with someone, their statements often trigger the internal thought of, "Oh, I need to say x or y when they're done." Like most of us, I love people and want to help them. In fact, most of the conversations I have often begin with the person seeking my spiritual guidance and wisdom. So, it's natural to want to foist my insights upon them when they come to me. I know this is wrong and I try to stop my interjections, but in the hopes of being polite, I stop myself from interjecting while also stopping myself from listening.

The worst sin of poor communication is that when they trigger that thought, I simply interrupt and don't allow them to finish their line of thought. "I already know where you're going and I have the answer. I can't wait any longer to get it out. You need to hear this." Far more often than I care to admit, my assumptions have missed the mark considerably.

℥ GOD'S INPUT

What I'm really doing at this point is seeking to interject my own thinking. I spend a lot of time listening to people but thinking about how I'm going to respond to their problems and what wisdom I hope to impart. They have come to me for my opinion and therefore I will do my best to express it to them. This is ultimately to say that I'm not really listening at all. But the Book of Proverbs has a problem with that. "A fool takes no pleasure in understanding, but only in expressing his own opinion," (Prov. 18:2).

The word "fool" in the Bible is a translation of the Greek word *moria* which means folly or foolishness, the root of which gives us the English word "moronic." Folly is directly opposed to wisdom in Scripture; it's polar opposite. Understanding wisdom as being that which is concerned with the preservation of life, foolishness or folly is therefore diametrically opposed to a healthy life. To be a fool, one is less concerned with truth and life and more focused on preserving self.

The temptation to express an opinion before fully understanding what the other person is saying has led to many negative outcomes. I'm sure you've experienced that yourself. The challenge that we face—to become good listeners—takes a lot of hard work and discipline to master. Let's explore if there is a practical tool to help us master good listening skills.

¶ PRACTICAL POINTS

So, is there a practical tool we can implement to put an end to our interruptions? Absolutely. At the Warrior Saints Movement, we work hard at something we call the *Three Second Rule*. It is a rule that is so powerful and can help us overcome our ineffective communication and listening skills. This beautiful rule was taught to me by my dear friend Mike Thayer. He's an amazing listener. He's so good at it that it almost makes me uncomfortable! The *Three Second Rule* is this: when talking with another person we must fight the desire to get our opinion in, to get our point across, to interrupt and . . . to pause for three seconds after they finish speaking. That's all there is to it. When someone is talking, wait three seconds after their last sentence before you respond.

This is brutally difficult for chatty people like me, but it is super effective. When implementing the *Three Second Rule*, so many beautiful things are happening. First, you may find that your conversation partner is not done speaking. If you wait for a count of three, there is often an uncomfortable silence. What do people normally do with uncomfortable silence? They fill it. Your partner will 99 times out of 100 fill that void with more thoughts. There's always more that they want to express. And if you're truly looking to discover the thoughts and struggles of a friend, give them a chance to tell you. The *Three Second Rule* gives them that chance.

Second, you show them respect. I know that when people are chomping at the bits to respond to me, they have not really grasped what I'm trying to say to them. They haven't listened to anything I've said. They haven't respected me. They haven't made me feel *felt*. But by listening with a three second pause at the end is as if to say, "I heard what you said. Your opinion matters." The Book of Proverbs goes even further and says, "If someone gives his answer without first hearing, it is his folly and shame," (Prov 18:13).

Why is it to our folly and shame? Because we have not allowed ourselves time to fully process and understand what is actually being said. This is the third part of the practical points in this chapter. By waiting three seconds and giving our brains a quick buffer, we can actually begin to process and fully understand what our conversation partner is truly trying to say. It allows us space to hear the story between the lines and get on the path of being a good listener. I'm sure you have had that experience when you thought to yourself, "Wow, they mean x," but when you say so, they respond with, "No, that's actually not what I meant at all." If you're like me, it happens far too often. Practice the *Three Second Rule* and give your partner a chance to tell the full story. It shows ultimate respect, humanizes them and allows them the chance to fully share their thoughts with you.

Go get some.

13

CRUCIFIXIONAL CONVERSATIONS: HOW TO TALK TO ADVERSARIES

In the first six months of 2020, tensions were on high alert in the United States and across the globe. The introduction of the novel coronavirus, COVID-19, caused great fear and divisiveness globally. Millions of people got sick and hundreds of thousands died. National and local economies were devastated when businesses were closed and quarantines locked people in their homes. Civil unrest exploded following the death of George Floyd by a Minneapolis police officer who placed his knee on Floyd's neck and assumedly suffocated him to death. Protests, riots and looting resulted in the aftermath and gave rise to renewed racial equality debates. The rise of the Black Lives Matter organization divided the country in half. As a result, conversations about defunding police departments split the country further. There were arguments about new types of public safety and about the idea that not all police are bad men and women just because of a few bad apples. Then, like a Phoenix rising from the ashes, COVID-19 made a comeback, creating endless debates on the efficacy of facial masks and whether they should be mandated or not. And of course, any discussion of the Great Divide of 2020 would be incomplete without mention of the political division that existed between Republicans and Democrats. No one likes President Donald Trump: they either love him or hate him. No one is lukewarm on Congresswoman Nancy Pelosi: she is either savior or devil. It was a particularly difficult time in America. Endless battles raged over ideologies, equalities and political positions. Social media platforms ceased being a space for conversation and connection and instead became battlegrounds for opinion and argumentation. Families and friends were torn apart.

♂ CRUCIFIXIONAL CONVERSATIONS IN CONTEXT

Regardless of your position on any of the aforementioned topics, one thing was made abundantly clear during the first half of 2020: people no longer knew how to communicate with one another. Any differing of opinion led to screaming matches and name calling. The ability to speak freely and have serious discussions were suppressed. Free thinking was deemed oppressive and cancel culture cost people jobs, businesses and most importantly, relationships. It seemed like no one had the ability to have an honest conversation anymore.

The main culprit was not the content of the conversations, per se, but rather the method of communicating. Listening to new ideas was replaced with self-centered monologues, openness was replaced with bias and fact was replaced with opinion. When objectively examined, the focus of conversation ceased to be about solutions or learning and instead became about "my opinion is right and yours is wrong." Conversations became about the propagation of self.

Contrast that to something I call crucifixional conversations. A very different approach to communicating with another person, crucifixional conversation places high emphasis on listening and placing the other person first. When conversations are self-propagating, they make the other person into a thing—an object—and no longer a human being.

If two things cannot coexist simultaneously, one of them has to be removed. And it's easy to remove a thing. Look, when someone becomes a thing—a democrat or a cop or a progressive—they're easy to smash. It's much more difficult to smash Tom or Sarah. But a thing is easy to attack. Conversing crucifixionally, however, is guided by the principle that this other person to whom I'm speaking is exactly that: a person. And as a person, he or she is made in the image of God and carries great value. I may not agree with the thoughts and ideas of the other person, but I cannot void them of their intrinsic value, and therefore, I better learn how to get along with him or her. Hey, you know what? Maybe I'll just have a conversation with her!

§ GOD'S INPUT

Chapter 4 of the Gospel of John recounts a fascinating conversation for us. In this particular story, Jesus had been traveling for some time and sat down by a well to rest. This particular well happened to be a famous well that the forefather Jacob had constructed. As any good disciples would do, the Twelve left Jesus alone by the well to go into town and get something to eat. It was then that a new character entered the story, the Samaritan woman (Jn 4:3-42). Samaritans were cousins, of sorts, to the Jews. Originating from the same twelve tribes that Moses led out of Egypt, their forefathers entered the Promised Land together and settled in their allotted portions of Palestine. Over time, however, the Jews (mainly referring to the tribe of Judah) and the Samaritans grew apart, even becoming adversarial. This was in part due to political boundaries, and in part, due to religious understanding of the Law. The two groups—though of common origin—became rivals. The Jews and the Samaritans basically hated each other[9] because their political and religious ideas were different. Hmm, kind of sounds familiar?

It is because of this that Jesus' ensuing conversation at the well was

---

[9] This animosity also makes the story of the Good Samaritan in Luke 10 so powerful. While the religious elite avoided helping someone in need, the "enemy" (in the form of a Samaritan), took care of his neighbor.

so striking. It was not surprising that Jesus was speaking to a woman. Jesus spoke to everyone. What is interesting was that He was speaking with a *Samaritan* woman. In some scenarios, we might expect the two to be at one another's throats, not engaging in dialogue. And yet, in John 4 we find an unlikely hero in the Samaritan woman, showing us how to have a crucifixional conversation.

Certainly, the main protagonist is Christ, but the Samaritan offers us some insight into how to communicate with others, even if we are from different worlds and have different mindsets. So that it's easier to follow along, below are the highlights from their conversation:

> "There came a woman of Samaria to draw water. Jesus said to her, 'Give me a drink,' for His disciples had gone away into the city to buy food. The Samaritan woman said to Him, 'How is it that you, a Jew, ask a drink of me, a woman of Samaria?' For Jews have no dealings with Samaritans. Jesus answered her, 'If you knew the gift of God, and who it is that is saying to you, "Give me a drink," you would have asked Him, and He would have given you living water.' The woman said to Him, 'Sir, you have nothing to draw with, and the well is deep; where do you get that living water? Are you greater than our father Jacob, who gave us the well, and drank from it himself, and his sons, and his cattle?' Jesus said to her, 'Every one who drinks of this water will thirst again, but whoever drinks of the water that I shall give him will never thirst; the water that I shall give him will become in him a spring of water welling up to eternal life.' The woman said to Him, 'Sir, give me this water, that I may not thirst, nor come here to draw.' Jesus said to her, 'Go, call your husband, and come here.' The woman answered Him, 'I have no husband.' Jesus said to her, 'You are right in saying, "I have no husband"; for you have had five husbands, and he whom you now have is not your husband; this

you said truly.' The woman said to Him, 'Sir, I perceive that you are a prophet. Our fathers worshipped on this mountain; and you say that in Jerusalem is the place where men ought to worship.' Jesus said to her, 'Woman, believe me, the hour is coming when neither on this mountain nor in Jerusalem will you worship the Father. You worship what you do not know; we worship what we know, for salvation is from the Jews. But the hour is coming, and now is, when the true worshipers will worship the Father in spirit and truth, for such the Father seeks to worship Him. God is spirit, and those who worship Him must worship in spirit and truth.' The woman said to Him, 'I know that the Messiah is coming (He who is called Christ); when He comes, He will show us all things.' Jesus said to her, 'I who speak to you am He,'" (Jn. 4:7-26).

Wow! There's a lot going on here, so let's explore it briefly. Jesus begins this conversation in a way that some may consider bossy. "Hey woman! Get me something to drink!" I know that when I try that at home, I get nothing but dirty looks. Obviously, the Lord is leading her to truth and salvation, but it's not hard to see that if spoken to like that in today's environment, she would have reacted harshly to Him. Instead, she responds with a question. Rather than initiate an immediate escalation, she uses the interrogative "how". Next, Jesus leads her further with the first hint of who He truly is, and again, she responds with a second question "where." The third question she asks about whether or not He's greater than "our fathers" allows Him an opportunity to speak and present His main point. After asking for the great gift of living water, she again does something impressive. When Jesus asks her to bring her husband—of which she was already done with number five—she doesn't hide her shame and she doesn't become defensive when he calls her out. She simply marvels at His knowledge, complimenting Him that He must be a prophet.

The Samaritan woman is a complicated figure and certainly carries her share of baggage. But the insights she reveals to us about crucifixional conversations are spectacular. In a possibly charged situation, she uses interrogatives, open-ended questions and compliments to gracefully communicate with a potential enemy. And thank God she did so, for by so doing, she not only found living water, but the very source of that living water Himself!

So, can we imitate her? In our own highly charged and volatile landscape, can Warrior Saints have crucifixional conversations with people with whom who we don't see eye to eye? You bet we can.

❦ PRACTICAL POINTS

Our practical points here rest on two very specific premises. The first is that the greatest aspect of having a successful crucifixional conversation is to listen. Let's define hearing as the physical auditory act of receiving sounds from an external source. Not much effort required on your part; you just have to have functioning ears. Listening, however, we'll define as an active process and one that requires much effort. It is something that seems to be dangerously absent in our world. To listen implies that we are searching for the meaning another person is trying to impart. That doesn't mean we have to agree with their statements. It just means that that we're trying to understand the point they're trying to make.

That leads to the second premise that is required for a crucifixional conversation, which is actually being interested in the thoughts of the other person. In other words, we're actually hoping to learn or grow from a conversation and not simply trying to win a debate. Look, unless you're a professional debater, don't enter every conversation with the attitude that you've got to be right. To be interested in and listen to the thoughts and ideas of another person, even one who could be deemed an enemy, is perhaps the one thing that can bring healing to an otherwise fractured world. Being crucifixional doesn't mean accepting lies as truth or opinion as fact. It means that we're setting aside an argumentative nature to hear another person out. It means that we're allowing them to speak so we can get somewhere. If after listening crucifixionally you disagree with a person's thoughts, you are certainly free—encouraged, even—to maintain your own personal beliefs. But how can you know if you disagree with someone unless you first listen to them?

Having laid down our two premises, to listen to and to be interested in another person, let's explore some practical points to help us become crucifixional conversationalists.

First, we come back to that beautiful and difficult rule to practice, the *Three Second Rule*. I know, I know, you've heard it before and are already working diligently on becoming a master of the *Three Second Rule*. But the rule is so important, I'm throwing it out there again as a reminder. In hyper-charged conversations, like those that dominated the first half of 2020, the ability to listen to another person and let them get their thoughts completely out would have served our great nation so well.

Second, by taking our cue from the Samaritan woman, the use of interrogatives is an essential aspect of having a crucifixional conversation. Starting questions with who, what, when, where or why are more honest modes of questioning. To start a question with, "did you…" is ultimately leading your conversation partner somewhere. Of course, in every conversation we are being led, but that's my point. You are leading them somewhere instead of following his or her lead to see where they go. If you actually care about the person you are communicating with, then it should matter to you what he thinks. So, allow him to tell you what he thinks, not about what you think he should tell you.

Third, and this is perhaps the most difficult of the three, look at the person's face. Study it. Even if you lose control over your listening skills for the moment, look at the person you are communicating with in the face. In fact, if you can, look into their eyes. Look deep into their eyes. I've found that when I do this, by examining the other person's face deeply, they start to become a person once again. Looking deeply into another person's face, I remind myself that God loves this guy. Even the most irritating people I encounter—and I encounter a lot of them over and over in my work—I'm somehow able to remember that this is a creature of God and is therefore of great value. It has also given me the important reminder that this person is broken and in need of love. It often dawns on me that the real content of this crucifixional conversation isn't so much about the words that they're saying but about the love that they need and the time that they crave. It's the human connection that they seek. Though they may be saying the words, "Your favorite political candidate is terrible!" what they actually mean is "Hey, I'm hurting, I need your love." Looking into someone's eyes you can see the hurt, the fear, the brokenness. Watch the corners of the eyes. As they turn downward, you'll know that the emotions on the inside are far more damaged than the words coming out of the mouth. Is the twinkle gone? Probably because the divine spark that enlightens them has started to dim. Or at least it has been smothered by the tragedies of their lives. Recognizing some of these cues, we cannot help but be moved to compassion. That broken and tragic person in front of me has become a person again, not a silly Republican that I have to smash. She's Sally again. And I can love Sally.

Go get some.

14

NOT EVERY CONVERSATION NEEDS TO BE HAD

Earlier this week I was sitting on my patio getting ready to watch Sunday Night Football. The weather was perfect, I poured a couple of fingers of a yummy single malt and my cigar was cut and ready to light. It was a perfect end to a pretty good day and I was going to cap it off with some smash mouth football. At that moment, my bride came out and said, "Hey babe, did you take the trash out?" I thought about her question for a moment. Man, that question has a lot of meaning packed into it. It could have meant any number of things. Perhaps she was saying, "Hey, you didn't take out the trash. Get on it." It was also possible that she was saying, "I have more trash for you to take out, so get on it." Or, she could have been signaling, "There's other trash throughout the house that needs to be taken out. Get on it." And of course, every man's favorite, "Dude, put a new bag back in the trash can!" But whatever it meant, it didn't mean what it actually means.

I was afraid of how to best answer her question. I didn't know the right thing to say. No matter what I said, I would not emerge unscathed from the exchange. In the immortal words of Admiral Akbar, "It's a trap!" Battling my temptation to respond with some pithy retort, I opted to do something rather surprising for me. In a brief and rare moment of clarity, I said nothing, paused the game and simply got up and went to the trash can.

You may be thinking at this point that this is clear evidence that my wife is the boss in our house. Nothing could be further from the truth. I am clearly in charge and she even gave me permission to say that in this book. Seriously. Who am I kidding?!

All joking aside, this cute little exchange between my beautiful bride and me serves as a reminder that throughout life, nay, every single day of our lives, there are conversations we get baited into that will end nowhere good. Nothing productive, nothing positive, nothing healthy will come from our engaging in them. And yet if you're like me, the temptation to respond is so great that we cannot help ourselves even though deep inside we know we're treading on dangerous territory. What we're looking for in this chapter is to come to the conclusion that not every conversation needs to be had.

⸎ NOT EVERY CONVERSATION IN CONTEXT

Social convention teaches us to be polite. Gentility is a quality that Warrior Saints hold in the highest regard. From early on in our childhood, we are instructed to speak when spoken to. But will we bear fruit by engaging in every conversation that comes our way? We all know that one person who always wants to bait us into losing conversations. For example, politics is the topic *du jour* that seems to push us to polar extremes. It can be such a divisive topic that brothers end up in fisticuffs if consensus isn't met. Or the temptation to be correct prevails over cooler heads and we find ourselves falling down the rabbit hole.

When we engage in these dangerous conversations, one of two outcomes usually happens: anger or hurt. And sometimes both. We argue our position in order to be right no matter the cost. We say things that are better left unsaid, causing hurt and damage to a friend or family member. Or, we feel embarrassed that we didn't say all of the things we thought of afterwards as we replay the exchange in our minds. By engaging, we've derailed our day with frustration, or worse, we've damaged a relationship with another person.

How do we stop this from happening? How can we live crucifixionally in those moments so as not to fall victim to the trap of useless conversations? I'm glad you asked! First and foremost, we have to recognize that nothing good will come from our engagement in this particular conversation. I know that sometimes we discover the danger of a conversation halfway through it, but most often, if we're honest with ourselves, we know from the outset that nothing good is going to come from what we're about to say. It is sort of like the story that started this chapter. We know deep inside us that we're treading on dangerous territory. Don't engage. Remember: not every conversation needs to be had!

ℑ GOD'S INPUT

Seldom read, the Apostle Paul's Epistle to Titus offers great insight into this topic when we hear the following:

> "But avoid stupid controversies, genealogies, dissensions, and quarrels over the law, for they are unprofitable and futile. As for a man who is factious, after admonishing him once or twice, have nothing more to do with him, knowing that such a person is perverted and sinful; he is self-condemned," (Titus 3:9-11).

Paul is exhorting us is not to get involved in senseless conversations because they don't work. And here, he is even referring to something as important as the Law. If avoiding factious conversations about important things is essential, how much more so about unimportant topics? Instead, take courage and politely admonish your conversation partner, reminding him that this particular conversation is going nowhere. If after having done so a couple of times he still persists, it is better to walk away than to continue to engage. Trust me. Even if you win, you lose.

℘ PRACTICAL POINTS

We have three awesome practical points to help us here. The first is a recap of something we hear throughout this book which is the *Three Second Rule*. Yep, here we go again. It's a difficult thing to do but it's so worth it. The *Three Second Rule* means that after your conversation partner finishes his statement, wait for a count of three before you respond. That's it. Three seconds. Seemingly simple, this is perhaps one of the most difficult things to do. Usually, we want to jump in and respond before our friend has even finished his statement! Aggressive language and inflammatory comments spark an immediate—and perhaps visceral—reaction inside of us. If we take the bait and respond in kind, then we are no better than our snarky friend. But if we can pause for a count of three, a few things happen. First, that three second buffer can enable us to process our thoughts, allow us a brief moment to decide how we will respond, or better yet, the foresight to see if we even should respond. Second, it shows respect to the other person, even if we don't agree with what they're saying. How many arguments could have been avoided if only a little respect was shown? Lastly, some statements are so absurd that if left alone to hang in the air, their true nature is exposed. Sometimes silence is the greatest witness.

Our second practical point is to reflect on how what you are about to say will be received by your conversation partner. It's not our place to hurt anyone ever. Look man, our calling is to respect every one of our brothers and sisters for whom Christ died (1 Cor. 8:11) regardless of whether or not they deserve that respect. That's a human being you're talking to with all of their brokenness and suffering. We're supposed to be Warrior Saints, to be crucifixional, so don't add to their misery. Instead of going on the attack, run your words through three filters before you utter them. Ask yourself if the words you're about to say are true, kind and necessary. Make sure your words meet all three of these criteria. Obviously, if they're not true you have no business saying them. Warrior Saints should never speak untruth no matter how tempting to do so. That means you have to overcome the temptation to say anything that you cannot absolutely prove. Next, if the words you intend to speak are unkind, then think twice about saying them. Being honest with someone doesn't mean you have to be rotten about it. We can always speak the truth in love (Eph. 4:15). Finally, is what you're going to say necessary? I don't mean necessary in that it makes you feel better. I mean necessary for the sake of the person with whom you're speaking. If he's walking to the edge of a cliff then by all means call him back. But if your words produce no value or will contribute to furthering an argument, consider silence.

Finally, practical point number three is to gauge the value of being victorious in the exchange. I mean, is it really worth it? Really? If you're defending truth, you've got to speak. You won't see me sitting by listening to someone tell me that Jesus is not the Christ. That's one conversation I can't leave be. Or if they want to take shots at my wife or daughters, they won't walk away without a response. But if someone wants to get hot and heated over why the Celtics are better than the Lakers, I'm not really interested in going down that rabbit hole. Not only do we all know that the Lakers are clearly a better team than their Boston rivals, but the content is subjective and ultimately of little value. Playful trash-talking is one thing. A full-blown argument risking friendships is something very different. It is not worth it to me to defend Showtime at the expense of a friend. Be self-aware enough to know if the content of a particular conversation is worth an exchange or is merely a small assault on your ego.

The best part of remembering that not every conversation needs to be had is that the frustration that goes with having them quickly vanishes. We end up with healthier relationships, more respect from others and a greater sense of peace in our lives.

Go get some.

15

FLAKES

July 1998 was one of the best months of my life. I had recently graduated from seminary and my bride and I were to be married in a few short weeks. We were going to Hawaii on our honeymoon before taking my first parish assignment to a wonderful community in Oklahoma City. It was a glorious time. Even planning the wedding wasn't quite as challenging as everyone said it would be. My mother-in-law, my bride and my mother had most of it handled. I was really just there as eye candy. I contributed when able and when needed, but I was more enamored with the grace and efficiency with which they planned all of the festivities related to our marriage sacrament. And our wedding reception was as regal an event as I've ever seen.

There was one thing, however, that left a bad taste in my mouth. Towards the end of the reception, Ally and I were asked by the photographer to come into the foyer to take a photo. We stood next to the table where all the cards with seating assignments were distributed. Typically, when you enter a wedding reception, you stop at a table and pick up your place card which has your name and a table number on it. When cocktail hour is over you find your way to the table indicated on the card for dinner. Pretty straightforward, right? Except that our table still had a few cards left on it. These cards weren't left over from people who knew where to go. They were cards left by people who didn't show up.

Normally, that wouldn't irritate me. Not everyone has to like me and not everyone invited to my wedding had to commit to attend. The problem was these cards were left by people who had committed to coming and then didn't show up. They were flakes! Thankfully, my bride is not only the most incredible person I know, she was smokin' hot that night (well, all the time really) and I was easily distracted from the irritation back toward our celebration. It was a much better headspace to be in.

I remember being agitated the next day, though, on the long flight to Hawaii. Why would people do that? Why say yes, make us plan for you and then not show up? Don't you know how hard it is to make seating charts for hundreds and hundreds of people? Don't you know that someone was left off the original invitation list to make room for you? Even worse, why did we have to pay for your meal and then let it go to waste?

I know, I know, first world problems. To be sure, in the grand scheme of my life, which has been filled with so many blessings, a few flakes at my wedding are inconsequential. There's even a wedding planning statistic that asserts six percent of your yes's will actually not show up. It happens to everyone. But it exposes a larger scale problem that we all have endured which is having someone commit to you and then flake.

℘ FLAKES IN CONTEXT

Every person has been flaked on in their lives. And I'm sure every person has flaked on someone else in their lifetime. Though it may seem trivial, I believe flaking is a serious crime in the crucifixional lifestyle. A lot of things have gone awry if you are flaking on another person.

First, your word is empty to me. I'm not even sorry for being crass. It's totally true. Your word means nothing to me anymore. You still matter to me, but I don't trust you. How can I? You say yes but your actions reveal no. When your words and actions contradict one another, I have no choice but to be wary of any promise you ever make.

Second, you have placed your inherent human value above mine. For example, if we set a lunch date that you flake on, you've essentially told me that your time is more valuable than mine. This is equivalent to saying that you're more important than I am. Time is our most precious commodity and we tend to spend the majority of it with people or places that are the most important to us. When you flake on me, you're effectively saying that this other thing that popped up is more important than I am. My perception is that you think my value as a human being is lower than yours. Come on, I said no to other people or events because I said yes to you. I was making you more important than me. My time is extremely valuable to me. I'm willing to give some of it to you, so let's make it count! Teenagers are notorious for being guilty of this one. When the day and time of the commitment draws near and they don't feel up to going anymore, their temptation is to flake.

Finally, you pansied out. If life as a Warrior Saint is focused on doing the hard things, of being comfortable being uncomfortable, how can we take the easy road out? That's really what flaking is. It's taking the easy road out. Warrior Saints just don't do that.

Think about how frustrated you get when your flight is canceled. What goes through your mind when your meal at a restaurant takes an unreasonably long time to arrive at the table? You're already thinking about flight coupons and free food. But then you expect others to tolerate the same kind of behavior from you when you flake? Warrior Saints are supposed to give to others what they expect for themselves. Actually, Warrior Saints are supposed to give more.

You may be saying at this point, "Yeah, Fr. Chris, but if you knew the real me, you'd know that that's not the kind of person I really am. The real me is not a flake." Could that be simply an excuse to make yourself feel better for doing something that you knew was wrong? There is no real you other than the one you give me. I can't crawl inside your head and discover the real you. All I have to go on are the actions you take. And if your words and your actions don't match, then invariably, I'm forced to label you as a flake.

❦ GOD'S INPUT

Flaking may seem like something inconsequential to God because in the grand scheme of things, a lot of serious and important things are happening. But nothing could be further from the truth. Jesus Christ himself is adamant that we honor the words we speak by making our actions align with them. In Chapter 5 of the Gospel of Matthew, He says the following, "And do not swear by your head, for you cannot make one hair white or black. **Let what you say be simply yes or no; anything more than this comes from evil**," (Mt. 5:36-7, emphasis mine). The message here is that making an oath or swearing to do something with words alone, such as committing to meet someone, isn't of any value. Even if you promise and swear on your own head, the words mean nothing if your actions don't align. The corresponding actions completed after making a promise or commitment either give the words credence or not. If the actions don't make the words real, the person who uttered them is simply not authentic. The only thing with which to truly know a person is his words. Words aligned with actions reveal the real you. Make them count!

A final example is helpful here. At my wedding, I was committing to my bride for the rest of my life. The word I spoke was a word I meant. I would be with her and love her until my very last breath. In order to give that word truth, I work hard each and every day to have my actions align with it. What value would that word carry if each day I was selfish and abusive as her husband? Would my marriage actually be crucifixional? I think you know the answer to that question.

❦ PRACTICAL POINTS

So, as we seek to leave flaking behind, what are some practical points we can implement to make our words and our actions align? What steps can we take so that we don't become known as flakes? First, if we commit to something—or to someone—then it is our responsibility to follow through with that commitment at all costs. That seems like such a simple idea, one that we don't need being reminded of. Yet, flaking has become such a regular occurrence in our modern context that I felt it required an entire chapter in this book. Other than death, nothing should keep us from following through with our commitments. I realize that sometimes legitimate reasons arise prohibiting us from keeping our commitments, but they are few and far between. Most of our excuses are exactly that. They are excuses. Being tired, having something better or more fun arise, no longer being interested, tardiness or other excuses are really revisions of the truth that we tell ourselves to feel better about poor behavior. Instead, sacrifice your comfort to make your words align with your actions. Being crucifixional is the real you.

Second, be very selective in the commitments you choose to make. When you are serious about making your words and actions align, it becomes imperative to ensure that you are making good decisions on what you commit to. I'm sure you've been invited to do something that sounded great at that moment but doesn't seem quite as attractive when the time actually comes. Instead of freely throwing yes around, take some time to consider what that yes actually entails. Spend some time in your calendar and see what your day and week look like. Ask for some time to get back to the person making the request. Keep in mind all of those times you said yes and then regretted doing so. By following these simple steps, it may become evident that you should being saying no more often than you do. Remember, every yes you say is a no to at least ten other things. Make your yes count.

Finally, hold your flaker accountable. Flaking is not acceptable behavior and it's okay to express that sentiment to the other person. You don't have to be rude, nor do you have to be a doormat. Use your skills of gentility and hold the other person accountable. When attempting to reschedule the date he flaked on, it is perfectly acceptable to politely suggest making a realistic plan, one that he can follow through on. And if the meeting is for business, it's also reasonable to remind him that you're beholden to other people (your respective bosses or clients). You might also consider confirming the appointment with the flaker a day before. Include language in your text or email, such as, "I'm leaving my office at 5:00 sharp, so I can meet you by 5:30." Show him the effort you're giving to the commitment. I bet you'll find he responds with equal grace.

Go get some.

16

YOU DONE WITH OPP?

P eople care about other people. Sure, we all know the guy who's only interested in himself, but mostly people want the best for others. It's probably innate to every man and woman on the planet that we don't like to see other people suffer. Of course, we all suffer, but we don't like to see it happening. And when we do see it happening to others, something kicks in that's powerful and almost overwhelming. When a loved one or friend comes to us with a problem, a desire to fix it seems to naturally jump to the forefront of our minds. "How can I help my friend fix this terrible situation?" Before we know it, we've committed ourselves to making another person happy and have become saturated in OPP (Other People's Problems).

The desire to help others overcome their monsters and face their fears is a noble one. It's a sign of love, care and respect for other human beings. We feel compelled to help them through whatever crisis they're facing and help them find happiness in their life. Like I said, it's probably an innate drive built into every human being. As a pastor, I know this better than most. People often bring their problems to me. "Fr. Chris, I'm struggling with this," or, "I'm suffering from that," is a daily occurrence in my ministry. And because I love them and want to see them succeed, the desire to want to fix their problems becomes almost overwhelming.

℥ OPP IN CONTEXT

The trouble with falling prey to this temptation is that we've placed ourselves in the position of being responsible for another person's happiness. And that's not really our job. First, as we have learned throughout this book, people need to face their own challenges. Our job isn't to fix everything but to help others live a life of the Cross in order to grow and mature. As difficult as that may seem sometimes, it is only through facing and conquering problems that we know that we're alive. Second, we have problems of our own that we should be focused on overcoming. None of this should imply that we don't listen, help, care for and love our neighbor when they are in need. If anything, by now you've seen that a Warrior Saint is always focused on sacrifice of self for the sake of another person. But being present to comfort and console a friend in need is not tantamount to actually fixing their problems for them.

℥ GOD'S INPUT

In the Gospel of Matthew, Jesus delivers the most famous sermon of all time, the Sermon on the Mount. Chapters 5, 6 and 7 are, in my estimation, the very climax of Holy Scripture. In these chapters, we hear the teaching from the Lord Himself on how to live a crucifixional life. Particularly important for us right now is chapter 6 verse 34. The context of verse 34 is a series of exhortations to ignore anxiety and worry. How we should dress and what we should eat are declared to be unimportant. Instead, we need only look to the birds of the air and the lilies of the field to see what a healthy focus should be. Birds don't plant crops, harvest and store them, yet God still feeds them. Lilies don't sew garments to wear, yet God still clothes them. And we are much more important than birds and lilies! Will not God also take care of us? You bet He does. So rather than worry about all these things, we are to seek first the Kingdom of God and His righteousness. Once we're focused on the Kingdom, the rest of our needs start to fall in line (v.33). The entire section now concludes with our verse which says, "Therefore do not be anxious about tomorrow, for tomorrow will be anxious for itself. Let the day's own trouble be sufficient for the day," (Mt 6:34).

Let's remember, this is not to say that we should ignore other people in their time of need. Getting through life as a Warrior Saint is something that none of us can or should do alone. We will only thrive as a community of brothers and sisters if we love and care for one another. But the responsibility to fix other people's problems is one that we have incorrectly placed upon ourselves. Our responsibility is to be present to listen and encourage our troubled friends through the crisis in their lives. To do more is ultimately to distract from their responsibility to focus on their current situation and make their own lives better.

ξ PRACTICAL POINTS

So how do we stay out of other people's problems and focus on our own? We have three practical points to explore: remember, move and pray.

One of the biggest culprits that lead us into the temptation of fixing other people's problems is forgetfulness. Not forgetfulness in the sense of our inability to remember facts. But forgetfulness in the sense that we forget that God is God. Not you and not me. I'm not God and you're not God. God is God. And we have to remind ourselves that being a savior is not our calling nor our responsibility. Because I love, the temptation is to fix the other person's problems, but God is the only true fixer. Because I love, my temptation is to heal the other person, but God is the true healer. Because I love, my temptation is to guide the other person, but God is the true guide. We have to start by remembering that God is the only one who will help guide, heal and fix our loved ones.

We do that in order to do practical point number two. That is to move out of the way. What I mean is that it is appropriate for us to let the other person fall sometimes. As painful as it may be for us to see our loved ones in pain, we have to sacrifice our desire to fix their problems and allow them to experience the pain of falling down and the victory of perseverance. We have to allow the other person the opportunity to be crucifixional. Think about the time you taught your child to ride a bike. Anyone who's done so knows how brutally difficult it is. Not because the concept is hard, but because you know that when you let go of the seat for the first time, the kid is going to fall and get bruised and scraped and bloody. But we do it anyway because we know that for the child to learn to find their balance and master bike riding, they have to fall. And they have to get back up. We should never rob someone of the opportunity to fail. Because with failure comes the chance to stand back up and overcome.

Instead, focus on practical point number three and pray for them. We should never dismiss the power of praying for another person. The Apostle Paul offers us a great example of praying for others' betterment in 2 Corinthians 13 when he says, "For we are glad when we are weak and you are strong. What we pray for is your **improvement**," (v.9, emphasis mine). Praying for another person is not like waving a magic wand that will solve all of their problems. Instead, we are offering our hearts to God on another's behalf, asking Him to grant strength, resolve and endurance. We ask that He might keep them focused on their goals and to never stop believing in the power of crucifixional living. And we ask that He might grant them wisdom so that His will might be done in all things. Pray often for your friends in need, but better yet, pray with them. How awesome is it when someone says they'll pray for you? Even more awesome is someone who will pray with you. Better than any fix, knowing that someone is on their side and is praying for them is oftentimes encouragement enough to stand back up and face the problem at hand.

All of this leads us to a bonus practical point of sorts. If we remember that God is the true fixer and move out of the way to let others face their burdens, while always praying for and with them, we will then have time to face our own problems. Facing our problems is what we've been called to do. The temptation to fix other people's problems is nothing more than a distraction from facing our own. And we have been called to let today's problems, meaning our problems, be sufficient for the day.

Go get some.

17

A GRATITUDE ATTITUDE

A rabbit was hopping along in the woods one day minding his own business when he came across a little village. He heard laughing and general good humor echoing from the little town, so he decided to investigate. The rabbit hid behind a little bush and what he found he almost could not explain! The town was filled with little blue creatures, called Trids, who were going about their day filled with joy and good humor. As he was watching those little blue creatures, he couldn't help but be jealous of their happiness and elation towards life. After watching them all day, the rabbit decided that he would return in the morning to watch how these little blue creatures began their day so that he could figure out why they were so happy all of the time. The next morning, the rabbit woke up before dawn and headed to the village. He got there and what he saw greatly disheartened him. All of the little blue creatures were angry and grumbling at one another. They were spitting, cursing and arguing amongst themselves.

Eventually the king, with his crown and scepter, came out of his house and all of the blue creatures stood in line. They were still angry and grumbling as the king approached the line. The king walked straight up to the first little blue creature and kicked him right over. When the little Trid hopped up, he was laughing and smiling and walked away. The king went down the line kicking the angry little Trids over one by one, wherein they hopped back up smiling and laughing. The rabbit watched for the rest of the day as these little blue creatures went about their business as happy as could be. The rabbit was confused but decided that in order to be as happy as the Trids, he had to be kicked by the king. So, the next morning he woke up early and headed to the town to find its inhabitants coming out of their houses grumbling and upset. And as the king came out, the rabbit hopped over to the end of the line. The king walked up to the first little Trid and gave him a kick that sent him tumbling down and laughing when he got back up. The rabbit was beginning to get excited as the king worked his way down the line. Finally, the king stood before the rabbit and looked up at him and said in a firm commanding voice,

"What are you doing here, rabbit?"

The rabbit timidly replied, "I've been watching your people for a few days and was wondering, first of all, what are you?"

The king replied in his thunderous voice, "We are the Trids! And Trids are a proud folk who do not take kindly to outsiders."

The rabbit, who was growing nervous now said, "I understand, King Trid, but I was wondering if you could kick me over so I could be as happy as all of the Trids in your beautiful little town?"

The Trid king looked up at the rabbit as a smile crossed over his lips and replied with rather good humor, "Silly rabbit, kicks are for Trids!"

⸋ GRATITUDE IN CONTEXT

Yeah, yeah, I know. Cheesy joke. But don't let the silliness keep you from hearing its message. Packed inside this trite little story, the tension between gratitude and envy is exposed. The rabbit, seeing the happiness of the Trids, became so jealous that he was willing to do just about anything to have that kind of happiness in his own life. Instead of deciding to be grateful for the blessings in his own life, the rabbit allowed his jealousy to so overwhelm him that he was willing to actively seek being kicked by the king.

The desire to possess what others have—jealousy—has consumed even the best of us at one point or another in our lives. When we look at the spiritual, physical, emotional and material blessings of others, the temptation to look at our own lives in an inferior manner can be quite strong. Rather than look at our own blessings and be thankful to God for them, we long to possess those same things in our lives. The imagination runs wild and we envision ourselves living incredible and carefree lives just like those who made us jealous. For example, if your friend Jimmy buys a new Tesla and stops by the house to take you on a ride, do you feel genuinely happy for him? Or is there at least a slight pull to think, "Man, I wish I had a Tesla Model X just like Jimmy. That would be way cooler than driving this old Honda Accord." Or imagine that your friend Candace has an exciting and healthy marriage that is the envy of your entire circle of friends. I know you say you're truly happy for her, and you are, but was there even the slightest tinge of regret for being stuck in a monotonous and loveless marriage? Further proof of your miserable life is written on the wall of every social media platform you use. Scrolling through your feed you see scores of people with seemingly perfect lives, always smiling and always happy.

When we allow jealousy to reign in our hearts there is a constant feeling of unrest and imbalance. And notice that I said *allow* jealousy to take hold of us. As we will see below, Warrior Saints have the power to decide to be aflame with the passion of jealously or to live with a gratitude attitude. If we permit jealousy to persist, nothing we acquire will extinguish the blaze aflame in our hearts and minds. There is always a chasing for more, to have more, to own more, to do more, to be more. This is a very clear indicator to me that a person's priorities have not been set correctly. We focus on stuff as the ultimate giver of happiness and in the end lose the clear-sightedness to see all of the rich blessings of our lives.

But the worst part is, if left unchecked, jealousy can morph into envy. At first glance you may think that jealousy and envy are synonyms, but I choose to define them differently. Jealously is the desire to have what others have. If Jimmy owns a Tesla Model X, then I want to have one too. Obviously, the error in this line of thinking is that your individualism is lost. However, envy is much more nefarious. Envy takes us to the extreme where not only do I want what the other has, but I'm willing to do whatever I can to make sure that the other loses it. Have you ever known someone who was so envious of Candace's healthy marriage that she attempted to sabotage it? Or worse, have you been the saboteur? In envy, our true humanity gets lost and rage prevails. We are living in our own personal nightmare.

℥ GOD'S INPUT

There is a terrifying story in the Book of Numbers. Seldom read, chapter 16 in the Book of Numbers tells the account of Korah, Dathan and Abi'ram. Known as Korah's Rebellion by Biblical scholars, a group of 250 men, led by Korah, Dathan and Abi'ram approached Moses with frustrations over his leadership. The context of Numbers 16 is that the Israelites were in the midst of a forty-year sojourn in the wilderness. God led His people out of Egypt and promised to deliver them to the promised land of Canaan. His servant Moses would lead them on God's behalf until they were given a land of their own.

Korah and company became disgruntled with Moses and the hardships of the desert. Gathering the assembly, they demanded that Moses be replaced. Confronting Moses and Aaron personally, Korah exclaimed, "You have gone too far! For all the congregation are holy, every one of them, and the LORD is among them; why then do you exalt yourselves above the assembly of the LORD?" (Num. 16:3). In the accusation, Korah was ultimately saying, "Why does this guy Moses get to lead us? Where have you taken us? You have done nothing good and it's time for you to step down. I, too, am holy and could guide God's people better than you have. I want to be the leader and a prophet to these people." His jealousy of Moses had become envy.

A challenge ensued at that point. Moses told Korah to gather in the morning and bring his censers filled with incense. Moses said they would swing them before the LORD and He would choose the holy one. God would decide who would be their leader. Moses said that if God chose him, the ground would split open and swallow up Korah (Cf. Num. 16: 16-31). Immediately after Moses finished speaking these words, the ground did indeed split open and Sheol swallowed Korah, Dathan and Abi'ram alive, along with their households. Interesting here is the mention of Sheol. An ancient Near Eastern concept for the land of the dead, Sheol is often conflated with Hell. Though actually distinct from one another in Scripture, to be swallowed up by Sheol and its fires is by no means a victor's end. It is torturous, painful and filled with sorrow.

Whether we read this story literally or not, the point is clear. Crushed under the weight of his envy and desire to be in Moses' seat, Korah was effectively swallowed up by Sheol. It's as if he was already living in Hell, consumed by envy. The story's conclusion of being swallowed alive by Sheol is to impart to the reader what our life will be like if we are envious.

ʃ PRACTICAL POINTS

So how do Warrior Saints embrace a crucifixional mindset and conquer the monster of envy? Let's explore three practical points to get us there. Say thank you, pay attention to the less fortunate and be generous with your blessings.

Remember the rabbit at the beginning of this chapter? He wanted to be like the Trids instead of being thankful for his own blessings in life. Instead of having an attitude of thankfulness for the forest that he lived in and the legs that he hopped with, he was envious of what others had. And he was insane enough to want to get kicked for it! All three of our practical points can only be successful if we first adopt an attitude of thankfulness. I like to describe it as having a gratitude attitude. Gratitude is not a feeling and it is not an emotion. Gratitude is a decision. It is a decision that we intentionally make to be thankful for all of the blessings in our lives.

Practical point number one is to say thank you. Common gentility teaches us to say these words, but how often do we do so with meaning? Has saying thank you simply become a knee-jerk reaction when someone does a kindness for us? Or do we deliberately embrace gratitude and then express it? Even more importantly, do we thank God for everything He has blessed us with? Remember, in the Epistle of James we are told that "[e]very perfect gift is from above, coming down from the Father of Lights," (Jam. 1:17). If every good thing we have comes from God, why would we not be effusive with our gratitude?

This morning I had my coffee outside on my patio. I've got a great house. I don't have the best house in the world, but my goodness, I have a house. I don't live in a hut or sleep under the stars like homeless people. I have a home with a beautiful patio and drink my coffee in the perfect Arizona weather. As I write this, it isn't hot and it isn't cold. It's beautiful. I looked out across my backyard and saw trees and cacti in bloom. The sun was shining and the sky was blue. The clouds were puffy and white. It was perfect. And I said, "Thank you, God." It was a decision I made to be grateful for all of the blessings God has given me. Say thank you and say it often.

Second, pay close attention to those less fortunate than you. Whenever you encounter the homeless, sickly patients in hospitals or those grieving the loss of a loved one, it is an opportunity for you to be grateful for the manifold blessings in your life. Warrior Saints don't look at those who suffer with pity but as a reminder of how good we have it. As tragic as I may pretend my life is, there is always someone in a much worse condition and carrying a much heavier burden. Would you want to swap places with that person? Seeing the suffering of others is an instant motivator for gratitude. Pay close attention to the less fortunate and be ready for practical point number three.

Practical point number three is to be generous with your blessings. The greatest advocate for a gratitude attitude is generosity. It seems natural that possessing more things would lead to gratitude, but the converse is actually true. Being generous is not only a sure-fire way to wind up grateful, but is also crucifixional living *par excellence*. Now that you've begun to pay attention to those less fortunate than you, give to them. Giving away our time, our money, our effort, our helping hands, this is crucifixional living. What's most fascinating about giving away is that we end up acquiring more. The knowledge of having done a righteous deed is more precious than gold. It is the ultimate slayer of jealousy and envy. Don't be afraid to be generous. I promise you, the more that you give, the more you will receive. It is an amazing truism that the more you give away, the more your coffers will be overflowing.

Go get some.

18

MARRIAGE

I n August 1998, my beautiful bride Allyson and I were married in Los Angeles. It is unquestionably the best decision I have ever made. She is an incredible woman with grace and strength unlike anyone I have ever known. Her physical beauty is striking, but her external beauty is merely a shadow when compared to the beauty of her soul. If there is one focus to her life, it is to serve others. Whether that's serving me, our children, or the countless souls that we minister to in our parish, she is singularly purposed to take care of people. The ease with which she exhibits her selfless love is inspiring to me. Her love is a great motivator to be the best husband I can be.

We've lived a fast-paced and awesome life together with a ton of ups and thankfully very few downs. There have been more highs than lows and more laughter than tears. Ministry in the Church, living in different cities and raising children have all been a wild and beautiful ride. We've been fortunate enough to take vacations to beautiful places. We've been fortunate enough to have great families and in-laws on both sides. The time I have spent with her is time I would not trade for anything on this earth.

No relationship is without strife to be sure, but we've been very blessed that whenever we do argue, it's really quick and really easy. We're both ready to forgive and forget and ask for forgiveness and grant forgiveness in order to move forward. Because of that, our marriage has been successful. We're able to do that because we are both unconditionally committed to sacrificing our own desires for the other.

℘ MARRIAGE IN CONTEXT

I'll get arrested for you baby. MLB pitcher Rich Hill was arrested and fined over an altercation with police in late December 2019. At a Buffalo Bills-New England Patriots game, Foxborough Police detained his bride, Caitlin Hill, from entering the stadium. According to reports, Caitlin repeatedly tried to enter Gillette Stadium with an oversized fanny pack. She was initially told that her bag exceeded size restrictions. Attempting to hide it in her coat, she made another attempt at another entry gate. Again, she was denied access to the stadium. After her third attempt at yet another gate, she was arrested on disorderly conduct and trespassing charges when she refused to leave the area when ordered by police.

I'm not really sure why the size of her fanny pack mattered nor am I interested in speaking ill of Caitlin. She's probably a fine person who simply made a bad decision. I'm more interested in what her husband, Rich Hill, did. According to the Boston Globe, "[h]e saw her as they were trying to get her into a van to bring to the police station, and he started to interfere with the officers. He was told several times to back up and he would not. And he ended up getting arrested."[10]

I do not condone obstructing the police from their duties. The service that those fine men and women offer to our communities will never be fully appreciated. They risk their lives every day to keep law-abiding citizens safe and out of harm's way. We all bear responsibility to heed their directions and guidance. But in this case, I applaud Hill for risking his good name and possibly his career—he was a free agent at the time—for the sake of his wife. He risked jail time, fines and possibly being signed by a new team to protect his wife. The incident was unnecessary, but crucifixional nonetheless.

---

[10] https://www.bostonglobe.com/2019/12/24/metro/rich-hill-acted-tumultuous-manner-toward-foxborough-police-leading-his-arrest-report-says/

I think he would agree with me that this was not the finest moment for him nor his wife. He was repentant for his actions, and yet he was still more focused on his bride than on himself. Hill's attorney released a statement on his behalf saying, "Despite Saturday's events, my great respect for law enforcement remains unchanged. However, seeing my wife handcuffed for a problem that started because of her fanny pack was extremely difficult for me to witness." Again, I fault him for the way he handled the situation. But I will never fault him for sacrificing for his wife.

§ GOD'S INPUT

The modern American landscape offers us the idea that if something is not perfect, just replace it and move on. We upgrade our phones, our cars and our jobs as quickly as a cat on a hot tin roof. We also abandon our marriages in record numbers. At the time of writing, half of all marriages in the United States end in divorce. Half. This is not only dangerous, it's devastating.

What is the cause for so much failure in marriage? Self-focus. The idea of sacrifice within the confines of marriage has virtually disappeared. Crucifixional living has been replaced with self-satisfaction, self-preservation and a false idea of perfection. Instead of putting in the requisite effort to better oneself, we blame the other person and bail.

St. Paul has different ideas on how to keep a marriage happy, healthy and viable. In his Epistle to the Ephesians we learn about the husband's role in the relationship with his wife. Rather than starting from a position of "how do I get mine," St. Paul pushes us to look at Jesus Christ as a model for a healthy marriage. "Husbands love your wives **as Christ loved the church and gave Himself for it**," (Eph. 5:25, emphasis mine).

You see, husbands are commanded by Christ to love their wives the way Jesus loved the Church, even unto death on a Cross. That means that as husbands, if we want to be the head of our families, we can only do so as sacrificial beings. Gone are the days of saying, "Hey woman, go get me a sandwich." Being the head of the family means that you are willing to sacrifice your very life—literally, if necessary—as well as all of your own desires for the success, well-being, happiness, love, joy, peace and comfort of your wife. To love your wife means that you must put aside your ego to give everything that she needs. It's sort of like Rich Hill putting his career at risk to protect Caitlin.

That doesn't mean that we give everything she wants. Not every desire is healthy. But outside of anything abnormal, our commandment as husbands is to love our wives as Christ loved the Church. At this point you must remember that love is not a feeling. Like is a feeling. Love is a verb. That means we have to be men of action (the word "love" in the Greek New Testament is most often conjugated in verb form). The Apostle Paul is telling us that to be in good, healthy and successful marriages, husbands must be crucifixional. We must sacrifice our needs and desires for the sake of the other, our brides.

Okay ladies, slow down. That doesn't mean that only your husband has to be crucifixional. Of course, the wife does as well. There are plenty of opportunities for the wife to submit to her husband. She doesn't get to snap her fingers and say, "Hey baby, go get me a sandwich." She has to be equally as crucifixional for her marriage to be successful. The message to husbands is equally applicable to brides.

The entire point of marriage is not to see what you can get out of it, but to see what you can sacrifice for it. That's the key to marriage. If both husband and wife constantly sacrifice for one another, I promise that you will not have a good marriage. You will have a great marriage.

⸋ PRACTICAL POINTS

How do we implement crucifixional living in our marriages? Are there some practical steps that we can put in place to treat our partner as the king or queen of our kingdom, our castle, of our lives? Of course, there are! The first practical point is that you must always respect your spouse. And that doesn't just mean at home but also in public.

Showing respect to someone doesn't mean that you defer to

everything that they want. Doing everything a person asks is not respect, it's helping a cry-baby get their way. Showing respect to someone means valuing their opinion, their thoughts and their desires. It means treating your spouse as though they are the most important person in the world because, indeed, in your marriage they are the most important person in the world. For the remainder of this chapter, we'll explore how husbands should treat their wives. But ladies, be mindful, every word applies equally to you as well.

Husbands, your wife must be for you the most important person in the world and you must treat her higher than diamonds, higher than anything, because she is far more precious than jewels (Prov. 31:10). To treat someone with respect doesn't mean there won't be arguments and fights, but man, we have to control the screaming, yelling, cursing and name-calling. None of that shows respect to the person we're married to. Likewise, it doesn't mean she's not going to push our buttons and make us want to snap. Wives are good at that, but so are husbands. We show respect because this is the person that we have chosen to show respect to.

Good husbands want to show respect in public as well. I'm always a little bit uncomfortable when I hear a man make fun of his wife in front of the fellas. It's something really strange to me. If I were to make fun of that man's wife in front of the fellas, he would be irate. How dare I speak about his wife like that? But why would I want to show her any respect if he doesn't? If a man has no respect for his wife, why would I? If he's willing to bad mouth her, that must mean that she's not really worthy of respect. That's also a testament to him because he chose to marry her! You will never hear me speak disrespectfully or belittle my bride. That woman is the most precious jewel in my life.

Practical point number two is to listen to her. I know that at the end of a long day, after hard work and a lot of frustrations, the only thing we want to do is come home and relax. Some days, the pressures of my life are so great that I feel like my head is going to explode. But there is a woman in my house who has been fighting her own battles all day, whether it be with our children or maintaining our home. Perhaps she has a job of her own and maintaining her career is equally as taxing.

At the end of a hard day she needs to have an adult conversation with someone who will listen.

I know that our tendency is to want to fix. If you're anything like me, you're a problem solver. You want to solve problems, especially for the ones you love the most. Very, very few things hurt me more than to see my wife struggle. When I see it, I immediately want to fix her problems. The thing is, she's a lot smarter than I am and is completely capable of solving her own problems in a far better fashion than I ever could. So then why does she need to talk to me about it? She needs to talk about it because women tend to think through their problems by expressing them. To use a terrible analogy, it's like a pimple. Sometimes you have to pop it to get the infection out so that it can heal. When my wife carries a heavy load from the day, her need is to get it off her chest. She does that by talking. My responsibility is simply to listen. I don't have to solve her problems, unless she asks me to, I just have to listen. My job isn't to correct her or tell her how she handled it wrong. I don't have to show her a better way. My job is to listen and be a support system.

Our third practical point as husbands is to provide for our wives. It's tragic to see how many men do not provide a stable home for their family. This is not to say that our wives could not survive on their own without us. That's hardly the case. My wife would be far more successful than I if she was in the work force. But because I love her, and because I am being crucifixional, I do everything I can to provide for her. You don't need to be the richest guy in the world and make millions and millions of dollars. Truth be told, most of us won't end up as millionaires. But it does mean that we have to do everything in our power to make sure that we can put bread on the table and a roof over her head and clothes on her back and a car to drive and insurance to keep her safe. To provide is our responsibility.

If that means you have to work more than one job, so be it. That means you have to gather the stones and say to your boss that you need a promotion. No matter how uncomfortable you may feel doing so. No matter what the challenges lie before you, it is your responsibility to provide for your wife.

Practical point number four? Date. Don't you ever stop dating your bride. You should go out on dates all the time. Why would you ever stop dating your wife just because you got married? You wouldn't stop calling her your bride just because you got married, so why would you stop dating? My bride is exactly that: my bride. Her being my bride didn't end on our wedding day. Even if I live to be a 100-year-old man, she will always be my bride. And you know what? I like dating my bride. So, I continue to take her on dates. Whatever it takes to make it happen, figure it out. Be spontaneous. Or make it every Thursday night. It doesn't matter to me how you do it, but never, ever stop dating your bride.

Lastly, be a man and say you're sorry. Look, I know we don't make a lot of mistakes as dudes, but we do make them sometimes. We can't be so arrogant to say, "It wasn't me. It was you." We've already talked about taking responsibility and not playing the victim and villain. Take responsibility for your actions. We all know that nobody's perfect. Nobody will go through life being perfect except Jesus Christ. Yet knowing that, we still try to defend ourselves as though we are perfect! Who are we kidding? If we know that we're not perfect, then we know we're bound to make mistakes. If we're bound to make mistakes, then we should apologize for those mistakes. Be big enough to apologize for any sin and any mistake that you make. It will carry you so far in the long run.

Go get some.

19

CHILDREN

I've been blessed with two daughters, beautiful young ladies, who make me a better man. I'm proud of them. I'm fascinated by them. I'm impressed by them. I love them dearly. They certainly do make me a better man. It is imperative to Ally and I that our girls know they are of great value to us, to the world and to God. We have worked hard to raise them to be faithful, ferocious, independent and strong leaders. They have not disappointed. There are indeed strong and ferocious while also possessing compassion for others and a deep, abiding faith in God. Clearly, I am biased, but they are the best kids on the planet.

I love to spend quality time with them and their mother. I simply enjoy them. One of the most enjoyable things that I do with my children is to flirt with their mother. They don't think it's funny. In fact, very often teenage daughters prefer not to see their father flirting with their mother, giving her a hug or a kiss, or embracing her from behind. I've often heard the phrase, "Baba, stop it. You're gross." I chuckle and my wife chuckles and we go on about our day.

On one occasion, my youngest had had just about enough of me flirting with her mother. So, she said, "Baba, you have to stop. This is terrible. I'm thirteen years old and I don't need to witness this kind of behavior." Funny girl! She was uncomfortable watching her parents flirt—I actually don't blame her!—and was politely trying to get me to stop. But knowing this was a powerful teaching moment. I turned to her and said perhaps the most important words I've ever said to either of my girls, "Do you see how much I love your mother? Don't you ever find yourself settling for a man who doesn't love you that much or more." The girls understood my message loud and clear.

℘ CHILDREN IN CONTEXT

As Warrior Saints raising children, our most important job is to teach them. We teach them manners, discipline, confidence, faithfulness and a relentless work ethic. We should also teach them that they only get what they earn while simultaneously teaching them to think of others before they think of themselves. It is also imperative to ensure a strong understanding of their value and worth as human beings. If we simply hope that they know how important they are without actually teaching them, it is impossible to expect they will realize their value and worth. And if they take a distorted understanding of their self-worth into their own marriages, they can end up in broken and painful relationships.

That is why it's essential we model how a man and a woman love one another. We can't expect our kids to just know how to love their spouse. They have to see how to do it. If we spend our time as husbands and fathers ignoring our wives, fighting with our wives, being disrespectful to our wives, what else will they know? Likewise, if we spend our time as wives and mothers constantly nagging our husbands, disrespecting our husbands, undermining our husbands, what else will our children think is normal? They will see fighting, disrespect and abuse as an everyday occurrence. That type of behavior becomes their normal and they will carry it into their own relationships. It is more important for us to teach our sons and daughters how to properly treat our spouse than anything else we can teach them. When they see a healthy and happy relationship, they will know exactly what to look for in their own lives.

I know that no relationship is perfect. My bride and I have the best relationship on the planet, but it's not perfect. We have moments where we fight, to be sure, but even in those moments, we're able to show the children what it means to be crucifixional within a relationship. We work hard to teach them the art of fighting in a healthy and constructive manner, not in an angry and damaging way. Children learn what they live, so let our children live as witness to healthy relationships.

℘ GOD'S INPUT

St. Paul's Epistle to Titus is a compact but insightful little letter. The letter is focused on teaching crucifixional behavior for the early Christians. In chapter 2 he says the following words:

> "But as for you, teach what befits sound doctrine. Bid the older men be temperate, serious, sensible, sound in faith, in love, and in steadfastness. Bid the older women likewise to be reverent in behavior, not to be slanderers or slaves to drink; they are **to teach what is good, and so train the young women** to love their husbands and children, to be sensible, chaste, domestic, kind, and submissive to their husbands, that the word of God may not be discredited. Likewise urge the younger men to control themselves. **Show yourself in all respects a model of good deeds**, and in your teaching show integrity, gravity, and sound speech that cannot be censured, so that an opponent may be put to shame, having nothing evil to say of us," (Titus 2:1-8, emphasis mine).

St. Paul is giving clear instructions here. He's asking parents and other older people to model and teach the younger people how to behave. This is precisely what we're focused on in this chapter. Remember, we cannot expect a person to know anything other than what they see modeled for them. To model what a healthy relationship looks like is fundamental to a Warrior Saint who is training the up-and-coming Warrior Saint. Show your children how to live and they will undoubtedly incorporate the behavior into their own lives.

⸎ PRACTICAL POINTS

Showing respect to your spouse should be at the top of the list. There are countless, practical ways to do so. Here are some of my favorites. First, gents, always open the car door for your wife. Every time we get in the car together, whether I'm driving or she's driving, whether we are leaving the garage or leaving a parking lot from dinner, I always open the car door for my wife. My girls have come to expect that I will always open the door for their mother. In fact, on one occasion I was distracted, deep in thought and I forgot to open the door for Allyson. My girls totally laid into me.

This practical doesn't end there. Open the car door for your daughters, too. When we drive to school or leave the mall, I always open the car door for my daughters. This seemingly simple and mundane gesture has tremendous power because it says to the girls that they are also of value to me. They, too, should be respected. Even though the task of opening a door for someone takes minimal effort and time, it sends a strong message: "I love you. You matter to me." I want my wife to know that she matters to me and I want my girls to know that they matter as well. Always open the door.

Practical point number two, as we discussed in the previous chapter, is to always speak positively about your spouse. We should never make fun of our husbands or wives. My family enjoys the playful teasing of one another, but we do not make fun of one another. Making fun of another person may seem funny in the moment, but it is always hurtful. Yes, we should be able to laugh at ourselves. That is a sign of strength and confidence. But let the jokes come from your spouse and not from you. No matter what we say or what face we put on, an insult even in the form of lighthearted fun can cause hurt and confusion. We question our motives, our value and worth when insulted. Part of being a Warrior Saint is learning how to transcend those fears, but for goodness sake, don't you be the cause of that for your spouse.

Equally as important is teaching your children to respect your spouse. As I mentioned above, we have a healthy and humorous family relationship in my home and we all laugh with one another when we do silly things. But at no point will Ally or I ever permit our children to disrespect us. Here's a true story for you. One day, when my girls were seven and five years old, they were giving it to their mother pretty good. They were young and as ornery as all little kids are supposed to be. She was going back and forth with them, negotiating a losing proposition. I smiled and waited while thinking, "Let's see if she can solve this." At some point I recognized that she was at her wit's end, so I decided to intervene. I raised my voice and said,

"Hey! Who is that woman?" They both looked at me and said,

"That's mommy."

"That's not mommy. Who is that woman?"

Again, they replied, "It's mommy." Tears were starting to fill their eyes.

"That's not your mother. Who is that woman?" I said again.

"It's our mom!"

In as calm and stern a tone as I could muster, I said, "That's not your mom. That's my wife. And nobody talks to my wife like that." They got the message loud and clear. The best part of the story? My little Amelia approached me after realizing how she was speaking to my wife. She said,

"Baba, I'm sorry I talked to mommy . . . I mean your wife like that." So precious! But also, it was so powerful to see that she knew I wouldn't tolerate anyone, including my beloved children, to disrespect my wife. You can be assured they will not tolerate that kind of behavior for themselves either.

Lastly, practical point number three is to engage them in deep conversations. Our children really are smarter than we give them credit for. I learned a long time ago that most children are way sharper than I am. They don't carry the crushing baggage of adulthood yet, and their minds are free and open to explore ideas in new and creative ways. Why would you not want to benefit from their insight? Rather than dismiss them as young and inexperienced people, set your pride aside and listen to them. It's amazing how often I have been positively impacted by their insights and intelligence. That's not to say that all their ideas are solid. Nor is that to say I stop teaching. We certainly don't negotiate. I am still the father! Rather, it's to admit that they have good minds and I want to know how those minds think. In our home, especially around the table, we spend an inordinate amount of time discussing ideas. Yes, some of our conversations are mundane and deal with the events of the school day. But most of our conversations are about serious ideas and thoughts. We want to engage their minds. Their thoughts and ideas are dismissed enough in their school and social media environments. If you want to show them that they indeed matter, give them a platform in your home to wrestle with complex and complicated ideas. They will be better because of it.

Go get some.

20

DON'T BE RIGHT. WIN.

People are born with a competitive spirit. We like to win. Actually, we don't like to win, we *have* to win. We want to win at everything. We want our favorite sports teams to win (as if we had any part in the Lakers winning another championship). We want our favorite political candidate to win. We want to win in our jobs. We want to win in the stock market. We want to win in our marriages. We want to win when we go to the casinos. We even want to win in driveway basketball against our kids! We're built to win.

As much as we love to win, we hate to lose even more. No matter how gracious we pretend to be, having to pay your buddies after a round of golf is the worst experience a man can have. Even if it's only buying the first round of drinks. And women losing an argument? The worst. The essence of humanity is to overcome any and all obstacles that we encounter in life. It is not sufficient simply to survive. We have to conquer. We have to win.

You might think that in a book about becoming a Warrior Saint the message would be about how to overcome any and all obstacles so that you could win. It absolutely is! However, in many of our relationship encounters we are willing to lose just for the sake of being right. Let me explain.

ꝰ DON'T BE RIGHT. WIN. IN CONTEXT

Many years ago, two of my staff members were in a heated argument. It was carrying on for days and days. He was wrong. She was wrong. He thought she was wrong. She thought he was wrong. In fairness, he did some self-examination to take responsibility if he was indeed at fault. But after the self-inventory, he was still convinced that it was her fault. Independently of her colleague, she also took the time for some self-reflection. Her examination also led to her exoneration. Consequently, their dispute kept raging on. At one point, I noticed that they had thrown each other into the penalty box. Just like in hockey when a player commits an infraction and is thrown into the penalty box, they locked each other away in an imaginary confinement where they refused to look at each other, refused talk to each other and refused to interact with each other. They literally became like ships passing in the night, working in the same space, but pretending that the other didn't exist. The effect was on its way to becoming potentially catastrophic to the whole team and the work we were trying to accomplish. It appeared as though they were only interested in being right.

I have made some mistakes in hiring team members over the years, but these particular people exhibited very high levels of maturity. Before I was forced to intervene for the sake of the team, they decided to reconcile with one another. The conclusions they came to in order to overcome their differences impacted me to the extent that I try to emulate them in my own style of conflict resolution. They came to the conclusion that they wanted to win.

One of these individuals took control of the situation and confronted her teammate before our weekly staff meeting began. The other team member recounted the story of reconciliation for me from his perspective: "She started with a loving plea to resolve the issue. She didn't want this to continue because we love each other and work well with one another. Thank God, in that moment, a weird sensation happened inside my body. My mind was waging an internal war with itself. I was trying to resolve two conflicting feelings. The first feeling said, 'I have to show her where she's been wrong. I have to show her that the mistakes are hers. I have to show her that the sins were hers. It wasn't my fault that this happened.' In contrast was the other feeling. One I hadn't really felt very often in the past few days of the dispute. And that was, 'You don't have to be right. Just win.'" After that, their reconciliation was complete within a matter of minutes.

I was super proud of my staff that day. They realized that the desire to prove the other person wrong was simply an attempt to protect their own pride. It had nothing to do with winning, finding a resolution or restoring harmony to our work family. It became about showing the other who was right. It became about preserving their individual egos. The cost of hanging on to their pride was detrimental to the entire team's success and they were not going to let that happen. As Warrior Saints, they both knew that to heal this situation required some crucifixional behavior. They didn't need to be right, they needed to win. And win they did.

§ GOD'S INPUT

One of the most difficult passages in all of the Bible is in Matthew chapter 5. In it, we hear the Lord showing us the pathway to harmony with one another when he says, "You have heard that it was said, 'An eye for an eye and a tooth for a tooth.' But I say to you, do not resist one who is evil. But if any one strikes you on the right cheek, turn to him the other also," (Mt 5:38-39). Though seemingly a simple concept, the famous "turn the other cheek" passage is so uncomfortable that most of us probably breeze over it without giving it much serious attention. The challenge of Matthew 5:38-39 is how it calls us to overcome the temptation to be right.

Think about it honestly. If somebody attacks you, confronts you or says that you're wrong and calls you out, what is the natural human response? Of course, the natural response is to lash out at them. To respond with anger and return blow for blow. We don't like being told that we're wrong. It goes against the grain of our precious egos which say we're right—we're always right—and we have to defend that by showing the other person that, in fact, they are the one in the wrong.

Jesus, however, is proposing something very strange in these verses. Whereas ego insists upon self-defense and a similar kind of response, a crucifixional mindset actually asks that we expose ourself to more abuse. That's right, expose yourself to more of their blows. It's similar to an ancient gladiator lifting his shield arm above his head. His core is now exposed to attack.

This should not be perceived as a call to being masochistic, but rather it is a call to win. The Lord himself is a perfect example of turning the other cheek (isn't He always the perfect example!). During His passion and Crucifixion, He was repeatedly struck, beaten, spit upon and mocked. How easily could He have proven Himself right. He is the Lord and could have done any number of miraculous things to show the Jews how mistaken they were. But His interest was not in being right, His interest was to win and to grant salvation to all mankind. And so, He accepted the goal of winning—not being right—and stayed silent during the assault of His oppressors. In doing so, He became the Lion of the tribe of Judah (Rev. 5:5) and won victory over Sin and Death.

♫ PRACTICAL POINTS

To emulate Jesus and keep walking on the Way of the Warrior Saint, we arrive at practical point number one. Unfortunately, it's about memory. Before we can allow ourselves to turn the other cheek, we must first remember that our goal is to win, not to be right. This is challenging because we're not only fighting the biological desire of self-preservation, we're also fighting the mental desire of ego-preservation. These self defense mechanisms go from zero to sixty in the blink of an eye. But what if we had a buffer? What if there was a way in which we could find a quick pause before responding? One tool I've found effective is to repeat the word "win" three times under my breath before I respond. Whenever I'm confronted with a potentially toxic situation, I simply remind myself to win three times before I reply. I confess, I have not yet mastered this tactic, but I am getting a handle on it. The more I practice, the better I become. When I say the word, at least two things are happening. First, I'm disconnecting from the anger the other person tried to provoke in me. Sometimes, simply breaking that connection is extremely helpful. Second, I'm reminding myself what my ultimate goal is. I'm reframing my context.

The second practical point is to master your impulse to talk or respond. As you learned from our chapter "Listen", when we jump into talking, we've jumped out of listening. Instead, be quick to listen and learn to ask the right questions. In any type of interaction, if we're trying to be right, we'll respond to every argument thrown at us with a counter-argument. We are going to return the attack. But if our motivation is to win, perhaps we follow the Lord's commandment and turn the other cheek. Stay quiet as Christ did in his audience with Pontius Pilate and listen as they throw blow after blow upon us. Listen and absorb them. I understand the level of difficulty here, but don't miss what's really happening. The other person is venting their frustration. All of the pent-up anger and hurt that they've been feeling is probably flooding out in a fit of rage. They will feel like they are being proven right. Let them. Remember, your goal is to win and heal the situation. If you listen carefully, you can hear their pain releasing in each and every stone they throw at you.

And then let them purge some more. The first assault is usually only an opening salvo. There's almost always a second wave. It's like when you pop a pimple. The first squeeze gets a lot of the infection out, but there's always more under the skin. If you really hope to win, let them get it all out of their system. That's when you find people to be more level-headed and open. Help them feel heard by asking questions. "It sounds like you're frustrated with me. How frustrated do you feel?" Another great question is, "And what else?" Give her an opportunity to get all of it out.

You're a Warrior Saint. That means your responsibility is to be crucifixional and absorb it and to turn the other cheek. You are now enlisted in the Lord's army and following His commandments! And here's the most beautiful part about all of this: when you do so, you are on the way to winning. Remember, winning is not about beating the other. That's reserved for sports. Winning in relationships is about peace and harmony.

Our final practical point in this chapter is to start practicing the art of apology. Very few tools are as powerful for healing as asking for forgiveness. Yeah, yeah, I know he may have started the fight. I'm sure he did. But like we said before, no one can fight all by himself. There is no Tyler Durden. If you are involved in an argument, *you* are involved in an argument. And if you have played any role in the argument, no matter how minor, you can apologize and ask forgiveness. Asking for forgiveness humanizes you. Instead of being seen as the evil opponent, with an apology you become Steve or Laura or Jim. In other words, a person. Opponents will attack. People can heal.

Go get some.

PART 3

MANKIND IN RELATION TO WORK

21

ONE THING

In the 1991 classic movie, *City Slickers*, three friends, Phil, Ed and Mitch, leave the chaos of their lives in New York City for a two-week vacation. On a cattle drive from New Mexico to Colorado, the three men set out to renew their sense of purpose. Throughout much of the story, the main character Mitch, played by the incomparable Billy Crystal, is at odds with Curly, the gruff cowboy who is leading the cattle drive. However, in one powerful scene, the two nemeses share an emotional moment riding along together.

"Do you know what the secret of life is?" Curly asks. Of course, the whole point of Mitch's journey is to find the answer to that question, so he plays along.

"No, what?"

"This," Curly responds by raising one index finger.

"Your finger?" Mitch asks confused.

"One thing," Curly replies, "Just one. You stick to that and everything else don't mean [expletive]."

An absolutely hilarious movie, *City Slickers* also holds a lot of life lessons for the Warrior Saint. The most important of which is taught in the exchange mentioned above. It is an absolute necessity to focus on only one thing in order to be truly successful. In a world that constantly pursues more, it's increasingly difficult to find that kind of singular focus. We're taught to make more money, have more sex, confirm more Facebook friends, take on more responsibility at work, complete more projects and find more free time to do what makes us happy. There's a funny thing, though, about trying to do more. We actually end up accomplishing less. It seems counterintuitive and yet it's so frustratingly true. When we engage in more activity, we end up producing less. But there's good news: the converse is also true. The less we focus on, the more we are able to accomplish!

֍ ONE THING IN CONTEXT

At this point you may be thinking, "Can't we get more done if we multi-task? If I'm doing more things in less time, then obviously I'll produce more." Welcome to the *More Syndrome*. And very little could be further from the truth. In a culture that constantly hopes to maximize our minutes, the myth of multi-tasking has taken a firm grip in the human psyche. But is there really such thing as multi-tasking? Or is multi-tasking simply our brain switching back and forth between two separate tasks. Because the brain is amazing and moves with such speed, maybe it only feels like we're doing two things at the same time?

Let's forgo the science at this point and run a little experiment to see multi-tasking in action. I want you to brush your teeth at the same time you're cleaning earwax with a Q-tip. At the outset, you may not see the big deal. But pay close attention and you'll probably notice that while you're moving the tooth brush back and forth—focusing on your teeth—you're not doing a good job of cleaning your earwax. So, in order not to gouge your eardrums, your brain quickly turns its focus to the Q-tip. Then you notice the side to side motion of the toothbrush starts to veer off course, so focus is diverted back to the teeth. Very quickly you discover that while I'm focused on one task, the other is not getting done very well. That's multi-tasking. Your brain is switching back and forth at lightning speed between two tasks. But neither of them is getting done very well. Or safely!

The message should be clear that in order to become great, to become Warrior Saints, we cannot get sucked into the *More Syndrome*. When we try to do more, we find ourselves spread too thin. More makes us the jack of all trades and the master of none. Instead, we have to find one thing to focus on.

℘ GOD'S INPUT

Once, an educated and zealous Pharisee named Saul had a powerful experience on the road to Damascus. While en route to capture more Christians for trial and persecution, Saul was struck by a blinding light. Knocked to the ground, he heard the voice of the Lord Jesus asking him, "Why do you persecute me?" (Acts 9:1-7). This was a transitional moment for Saul. It led to a three-day period of solitude and fasting, followed by a name change and a new mission to carry the Lord's name before the Gentiles, kings and the sons of Israel (Acts 9:15). In other words, now that he had become the Apostle Paul, his one thing was to preach the Gospel of Jesus Christ to the nations. And preach the Gospel to the nations he did! St. Paul's ministry bore tremendous fruit in the Gentile world and it still stands to this day as the root for nearly all Christians. His writings comprise the bulk of the New Testament and he is read every day, in every Christian denomination throughout the world.

Not surprising, in one of his communities, Corinth, disputes and dissension arose in the mid-first century. In this particular community, discussion arose over who was the ultimate progenitor of their local church. Some claimed that they belonged to Paul. Others claimed to belong to another preacher, Apollos. While still others claimed to belong to Cephas (referring to the Apostle Peter). And perhaps the smartest faction claimed to belong to Christ. St. Paul quickly dispelled any misunderstandings by reminding them that Christ is not divided, and to "belong to Him" means that the Corinthian Christians cannot be divided either (1 Cor. 1:10-17). The most fascinating part of this section, however, comes after St. Paul chides the Corinthians for their division by saying, "For Christ did not send me to baptize but **to preach**

the gospel, and not with eloquent wisdom, lest the Cross of Christ be emptied of its power," (v.17, emphasis mine).

Christians believe that baptism is the rite of initiation into the Faith. Regardless of the denomination to which one belongs, it is universally agreed that by being baptized into Christ,[11] one becomes a Christian. In the Orthodox Church, we teach that one becomes a child of God, a child of the Kingdom, in and through baptism. Further, the New Testament makes it clear that in baptism, we are clothed with Christ (Gal. 3:27) and share in the death of Christ (Rom. 6:3) with the chance to walk in the newness of life. To say that baptism is optional for a Christian would be a gross understatement at the very least. Baptism is the birth of the Christian. It is what sets us on the path towards a Christ-like life. It is the beginning of the Warrior Saint.

So why would the great apostle not be concerned with baptizing people? Sure, he admits to baptizing a few people in Corinth, but only after offering the caveat that he's glad he hasn't done very many. For someone trying to grow the fledgling Christian community, he sure seems hesitant to perform the very act that brings one into the Body of Christ. The question follows then, is Paul missing it? Did he miss the high nature of his calling? Or, perhaps, contrary to the idea of doing multiple tasks, he recognized that Christ commissioned him with one thing which was to preach the Gospel. Others could baptize. His focus was preaching. And he was going to focus on it relentlessly.

℘ PRACTICAL POINTS

The movie scene from *City Slickers* noted above has an amazing conclusion. After Curly reveals that the secret to life is only one thing, Mitch replies in a defeated tone,

"Yeah that's great, but what's the one thing?" The height of the

---

[11] Some denominations understand baptism as immersion in water while others understand it as immersion of belief. Either way, the concept of baptism is essential to initiation into the Christian Faith.

movie's message is revealed by the most unlikely of heroes. The gruff and wizened old cowboy simply points his finger at Mitch and says,

"That's what you've gotta figure out." Mitch's journey was not to drive cattle from one place to another, it was to discover what was the one thing in his life. No one could tell him the answer. It was something only he could discover.

If you often feel like Mitch, it's time for you to begin the search for your one thing. Since we're in the chapters devoted to our relationship to work, we'll stay focused on business and work-related topics. But know that finding and focusing on your one thing is as equally important in your spiritual life, with your family, in physical and mental health. Focusing on one thing can be applied to every aspect of your life.

Our practical points in this chapter are extremely important. You've got to start by finding the one thing that's truly your own. What is that one thing that you will attempt to master? What is the one thing that you can be better at than anyone else on the planet? What contribution will you give to the world? Only you can find the answer. The first practical point to help you do so is *The Focusing Question*[12]. In *The ONE Thing*, which I consider to be an essential read, authors Gary Keller and Jay Papasan formulate a simple question that helps anyone dig deep enough to find their one thing. They call it *The Focusing Question*. I strongly recommend you read *The ONE Thing* and let Keller guide you in the art of using *The Focusing Question*. But to get a head start, the question is, "What's the one thing I can do, such that by doing it, everything else becomes easier or unnecessary?"[13]

Here's how it works. Take as an example one of the projects that you have going on at work. Let's say you've got a major sales presentation to make to a potential client. This client is very important to your bottom line, but he has a reputation of being difficult to persuade. So, start by asking yourself *The Focusing Question*. "What's the one thing I can do to make this sale easy to close?" Your answer should be to learn exactly what the client needs so you can show how your product fills that need.

---

[12] Keller, Gary, *The ONE Thing*. Page 103.
[13] Ibid, pg.106.

Now ask *The Focusing Question* again. "What's the one thing I can do to discover my client's need?" Now you turn your attention to discovering where his business is not as successful as it should be. Ask the question again, "What's the one thing I can do to help him be successful?" By repeating this process, you are sure to drill down to find the one thing you need to do in order to close the sale.

Though this example may seem banal, it shows how utilizing *The Focusing Question* cuts through the mire of an infinite number of ancillary activities. As we keep asking the question, we get closer and closer to finding the one thing we're trying to accomplish. How many times do you repeat *The Focusing Question* to get to your one thing? I guess the answer depends on how big a task you've got in front of you. Easier tasks obviously need less iteration while more important goals may require more. I've rarely gone beyond five.

Practical point number two is to make sure you safeguard the time needed to accomplish your one thing. As we've already seen in this book, a lot of distractions are competing for our time. Chaos is just waiting to destroy your plans. Take control of your time or lose it.

Have you ever woken up with a gung-ho attitude, knowing that you're going to knock it out of the park today? You've got this one major task that you really need to get done and you're super motivated and chomping at the bits to get after it! The whole drive to work is exciting and you're planning what steps you'll implement to get rolling on your one thing. It's such a good feeling. And then it happens. You already know what I'm going to say. You walk into your place of work and the world explodes around you. Everyone has emergencies at that very moment. Emails pound your inbox with endless requests. The copy machine breaks down, someone wants to gossip with you at the water cooler, your phone never stops ringing. By the time you end up laying down to sleep, you think to yourself, "How did this day happen? I didn't get anything of real value done, most importantly that one thing I was so excited for at the start of the day!" We've all had those days, and you know what? They only happen when you don't have time for them to happen. It's Murphy's Law I guess, but it's totally true. Just when things feel like they're rolling, it all comes tumbling down with mundane distractions.

It's impossible to avoid days like that. They've happened to us all and they will happen again. So, you can submit and allow those days to commandeer your morning, or you can safeguard your one thing by ignoring the chaos. Let me explain what I mean. For years I have been allocating specific periods of time in my schedule to attack my big goal and to do my one thing. It dawned on me in the early years of my ministry that I can't control the chaos. It will always find me. But I can control if I react to it. And my chunks of time set aside to work on my one thing are sacrosanct. It is sacred time that is for one thing only. No phone calls, no email, no water cooler gossip, no broken copiers, no emergencies. During that scheduled time period, I only work on my one thing. Even my bride has to leave a message! I try never to go to sleep at the end of the day feeling like I accomplished nothing. If I get my one thing done during that sacred time period, then I know, even if not my best work, I got some real work done. Once that sacred time is complete, I am free to focus on the myriad emergencies waiting to be managed.

Now that you know you've discovered your one thing by using *The Focusing Question* and have committed to the idea of sacred time to work on it, it's time for practical point number three. Deliberately set quality blocks of time to focus and work. Saying you will dedicate time to your one thing is vastly different than actually scheduling time for your one thing. If it's important to you, schedule it. So, when do you schedule your sacred time? The answer is really up to you but make sure it is when you are at your very best. After a long day of teaching, writing and managing a thriving parish, my brain is pretty much empty. To sit down at that point and try to write a solid chapter is just not going to happen. Trust me, I've tried.

The morning is when my brain is at its freshest. I wake, say my prayers, drink some coffee and then exercise. The big three are done! With my brain caffeinated and my blood flowing, I am ready to do some serious work. I have scheduled a repeating two-hour block appointment in my calendar to focus on my one thing. In that span of time, nothing else gets my attention but deep work. I do not schedule anything else during those two hours and I don't allow my assistant to do so either. It's just me and my work. You're reading this book because of that dedicated time. You may find different times during the day when you are at your best. Just make sure to use those times to do your most important work.

Go get some.

22

COMMITMENT

Michael Phelps is the most decorated Olympian of all time. He won a total of twenty-eight medals spanning five different Olympiads. His accomplishments become even more impressive when you consider the fact that in 2000, his first Olympics, he finished in fifth place in his only race. In the next four Olympic Games, Phelps earned twenty-three gold, three silver and two bronze medals. Beijing in 2008 proved to be his *coup de grâce* as he went 8-for-8 in his races, winning eight gold medals. He broke the world record for most golds in one Olympiad, passing fellow American, Mark Spitz, who won seven first place finishes in 1972.

What lifted Phelps from zero Olympic wins in 2000 to complete domination for the next sixteen years? His age could certainly have been a contributing factor. In the 2000 Olympics, he was only fifteen-years old, the youngest U.S. Olympic swimmer in sixty-eight years. His young body, not fully developed, competed against older, stronger and more experienced swimmers. As he grew over time, his frame developed into the physical specimen we all remember. He also enjoyed a support system that aided his success. His mother Debbie and two sisters forced him to begin swimming at age seven. He fell head over heels in love with the sport and was encouraged by his family until his retirement in 2016. And of course, he had an excellent coach. Bob Bowman was a prolific swim coach and already enjoyed gold medalists in his club. His ability to challenge and push Michael led to a razor-like focus in the pool.

All of these factors were important to Phelps' success, but more than anything else, his commitment to winning took him over the top. Phelps recounts that after losing in 2000, he became obsessed with winning every single race he entered. He wanted to win, and he also *committed* to winning, setting aside all else to focus on that goal. It is said that before the 2004 Olympics, Phelps was training every day. Every day as in seven days a week, fifty-two weeks a year, 365 days in a row. There were no Thanksgiving holidays nor Christmas breaks. He was in the pool every single day. And in those days, he only did three things: eat, train and sleep. That's it. No football, no video games, no parties, no traveling. He was so committed to winning gold medals that he literally did nothing else. He made no excuses, got into the pool and started swimming. The result? Twenty-eight Olympic medals.

⸹ COMMITMENT IN CONTEXT

In similar fashion, Warrior Saints are born in the fire of commitment. We have been called to transform ourselves from something mediocre into something special. Each of us has goals and desires and dreams that could impact the world in positive and powerful ways. So why don't we see them come to fruition very often? Why are we not committed to transformation today? Why do we miss out on the many blessings that we have to offer to our brothers and sisters in the world? We miss out because of the *Tomorrow Syndrome.*

The *Tomorrow Syndrome* is a common enemy that plagues so many of us. Instead of jumping quickly into action to complete—or even begin—our goals, we rest easy based on the promise that we'll start tomorrow. How many times have you promised yourself you'll start tomorrow? I will absolutely begin my diet for real tomorrow. I will totally start exercising on January 1st. I'm going to write my paper or presentation well before it's due so I can review it. I'm going to change how I behave towards my spouse and children. I'm going to write my chapter on commitment for a book. I'm going to ask for forgiveness from that person I hurt. I'm going to build my small business into an empire. I will wake up early and praise God.

Could your list go on? Mine sure could. The *Tomorrow Syndrome* is a powerful force that tempts us to sacrifice long term success for comfort in the moment. We are reminded that all of the work we face today will still be waiting for us tomorrow, so no need to start it now. Just rest and relax today. And then what happens? Our diet becomes just one more cookie and a bag of Doritos. Our exercise becomes another quick binge on Netflix. Our paper is mediocre at best because it got pushed until the night before the deadline. Bitter behavior towards your spouse and children sediments deeper into bad habits. Chapters don't get written, forgiveness never sought, businesses flounder and God doesn't hear the sound of our praise. We find ourselves locked in the miry bog of mediocrity.

You know those before-and-after photos where we see someone who has transformed his life by losing a lot of weight? We all like the after-photos. Seeing someone's transformation is inspiring and motivating. Whenever I see one of those photos, I'm committed to working out and getting my abs back. Like legit, this time I'm going to get them back. And then I'm confronted with the process. Then I have to look the hard work of exercise and diet square in the eyes. My commitment to transformation wanes. And tomorrow becomes an easy promise.

℥ GOD'S INPUT

Fear not, this is not a new phenomenon. Mankind has been procrastinating since the dawn of time. God knows that we all like the after-photos but are not so thrilled about the process it takes to get there. He also knows that without the process, there is no after-photo. So how does He bring the dread of the process together with the joy of the results? By teaching us to just start!

In an agrarian society, missing the deadlines of seed planting can be devastating to a healthy harvest. If the seeds are not planted at the right time, when harvest season comes, the crops will not be fully grown or may not even exist. The farmer knows that if he wants to eat during the winter, he's got to get up early, plant his seeds in the right season and tend to the crops throughout the growing months. He can't just desire bread in the winter. He has to go through the process of growing his wheat if he's going to eat all year long. He's got to be committed to the entire process! In Proverbs, God encourages us to take that idea seriously: "The soul of the sluggard craves, and gets nothing, while the soul of the diligent is richly supplied," (Prov. 13:4). Craving the after-photo isn't going to get it done. In fact, the craving will actually get you nothing. It's through the *process* that we achieve our goals. It's only by being committed to transformation and doing the hard work, that we will see the results. By being committed to wrapping ourselves in the cocoon of focus, dedication and disciplined effort, we will see the results we seek. Waiting until tomorrow doesn't work. We simply have to start!

℘ PRACTICAL POINTS

Our first practical point is to stop making excuses. I'm a master at excuse making. I can find a gazillion excuses to not finish this chapter. As I write these words, I'm overwhelmed with the *Tomorrow Syndrome*. Writing isn't my strong suit and I don't like doing it. And there are a million distractions actually happening right now that could be an excuse to stop writing. Emails from parishioners, a death in the parish, prepping for an upcoming baptism tomorrow, doing my exercise, hanging with my bride and daughters, jumping in the pool, calling my mom to check in, and on and on. I am tempted by the myriad of possible excuses to write this chapter tomorrow. There will always be more interesting and easier things to draw you away from doing the hard work to which you are committed. In order to just start, you have to stop allowing the excuses to creep in. See them for what they are: excuses and distractions. It's almost as if the devil doesn't want you to accomplish your goals, so he taunts you with more interesting and fun tasks. Don't bite.

The second practical point is to write a plan. I know, I know, here we go again with plan writing. Believe me, I get it. Plan writing has never been an interest of mine either nor a tool I'm fond of using. But as I was experimenting for the writing of this book, I thought, why not, let's give it a shot. And something beautiful happened. Seeing the plan for the book made it appear so much more possible. To tell yourself you're going to write a book and then sit down and type it is a kind of a strange approach. It gives no sense of time, no milestones to reach, no cohesion to the chapters and an overwhelming sense of the magnitude of the task. But when a plan is drafted that delineates your thesis, your book sections, the chapter titles for each section, the ideas for each chapter and the day you will work on each chapter, that daunting feeling seems to vanish. Writing a book becomes real. There are a lot of wonderful tools to help you write your plan and I recommend you take advantage of them. I suggest starting at *12weekyear.com*. The *12 Week Year* is an idea taught by Brian Moran and Michael Lennington that compacts a year's worth of effort and work into a 12-week cycle. You should check it out.

The final practical point of this chapter is simply to start. Not exciting, I know. But so powerful. If you wait for inspiration to lead to action, you're done. The converse is actually true. Action leads to inspiration. The promise of action is far less impressive than actual action. Giving a hundred percent tomorrow is half as effective as giving fifty percent today. We may not get tomorrow, so make it count today. I use little tricks to get myself going. For example, to write, I commit to writing only 400 words. That's it, 400 words. On my laptop, 400 words is about one and a half pages doubled-spaced. There are very few days that I'm so busy I don't have time to write a page and a half. But something interesting happens when I start. Those 400 words quickly become 1000. And 2000. And a chapter.

Something similar happens when you struggle to do your exercise. Telling yourself that you're going to run five miles today may seem daunting. So, commit to only a half a mile. That's it, half a mile. Funny how by the time you get to that half mile marker, your blood is flowing and you're juiced to get some more. But you wouldn't have gotten your five miles in if you didn't just start.

The ideas in the chapter are really simple and don't take an expert to figure them out. Yet so many of us fail to do them with regularity and commitment. By promising ourselves that tomorrow will be the day we get after it, we miss opportunities to make an effective difference in the world today. Too many tomorrows add up to no fruit.

Go get some.

23

TIME

There is a marvelous little metaphor often shared in self-improvement or time management seminars. The speaker begins with an empty jar and then proceeds to place some large rocks inside. Once the rocks reach the top of the jar, he asks if the jar full. The participants who have never seen this experiment answer quite enthusiastically, "Yes!" Smiling, the presenter pulls out another jar filled with gravel and pours the contents into the first jar. Sliding between the big rocks, the gravel works its way to the bottom until it, too, reaches the top of the jar. Again, the presenter asks if the jar is full. This time, with slightly more skepticism, the attendees respond with, "Yes." Again smiling, he pulls out a bucket of sand and pours it into the jar with the rocks and gravel. The sand, smaller than the gravel, works its way into all the nooks and crannies. Once it reaches the top, the presenter once again asks his question. This time, the crowd, beginning to recognize his trickery says, "No!" With a final smile, he then pours a glass of water into the jar, completely filling all of the remaining empty space.

When the trainer asks the participants what message he's hoping to convey with this experiment, it is not uncommon to hear people respond with, "Well, there are gaps, and if you work hard, you can always fit more things into your life." Then the trainer drops the bombshell:

"No, that's not really the point. The point is to put your big rocks in first."

℥ TIME IN CONTEXT

In a hyper-connected world, we can communicate with another person in a multitude of ways. Phone calls, email, text messaging, WhatsApp, Facebook and Messenger, Instagram, TikTok, Snapchat, LinkedIn to name but a few of the most common. It's a blessing to have so many tools to connect us with other people. However, along with all the means of communication come notifications for each of them. Rings and chimes telling you when someone liked your post, liked your photo or sent you a Snap are regular occurrences throughout one's day. And almost every job, whether working in an office or on an assembly line, produces a senseless quantity of emails that are constantly bombarding our inboxes.

Something dangerous accompanies these connection tools. Instead of simply enhancing the ability to connect, they have become major distractions, wasting our precious time in non-essential tasks. We've learned to put the sand and the gravel into the jar of our lives first, leaving little room, if any, for the big rocks.

Have you been working at your desk on a report or project that needed to be completed as soon as possible only to have your attention diverted by a chime from Instant Messenger on your laptop? Did your significant other send you a Snap with a cute dog nose and a flower halo? Did your boss send you an email with another task for you to complete? Have you been swallowed up by the vortex that is YouTube surfing? If you have a cell phone, you know exactly what I'm talking about and have experienced the collapse of quality time. There are countless scientific studies available to discern the harm of this phenomenon. Most interesting to me are the studies that indicate that even looking quickly at an email costs anywhere from five to seventeen minutes to refocus on what you were originally doing (depending on the study you read). If we split that number in half and say it only takes ten minutes to refocus, six emails can ruin the entire hour you set aside to work on your project. Six emails. That's all it takes to ruin an entire hour. I know we all get six emails an hour. If we're lucky, it's only six.

⸎ GOD'S INPUT

Though only one small example of the many distractions we face, notifications tickle the subconscious mind and distract you from doing the important things you want to do. God, however, is particularly interested in seeing us pay attention to our big rocks. He's looking for us to use our time wisely and live crucifixional lives. Chapter 3 of Ecclesiastes says it well, so well that Pete Seeger of the Byrds used half the chapter in his 1962 hit, "Turn, Turn, Turn (To Everything There is a Season)." It goes like this:

> "For everything there is a season, and a time for every matter under heaven: a time to be born, and a time to die; a time to plant, and a time to pluck up what is planted; a time to kill, and a time to heal; a time to break down, and a time to build up; a time to weep, and a time to laugh; a time to mourn, and a time to dance; a time to cast away stones, and a time to gather stones together; a time to embrace, and a time to refrain from embracing; a time to seek, and a time to lose; a time to keep, and a time to cast away; a time to tear, and a time to sew; a time to keep silence, and a time to speak; a time to love, and a time to hate; a time for war, and a time for peace," (Eccl. 3:1-8).

It's an amazing text to be sure and the simplicity and clarity make it accessible for any reader. Notice that at no point does the author mention notifications. This is not an attempt at humor, but rather to recognize that nowhere in this list do we find the mundane. Birth, death, love, war, peace, healing and building are all essential ideas. It seems we're being told to use our time to do the most important things. I don't know, it's kind of like putting our big rocks in the jar first. Time is a finite resource and our most precious commodity. Each of us has been given twenty-four hours—86,400 seconds—per day and we should make them count. Many outside influences will try to distract and usurp our time. It is our job to protect it.

℘ PRACTICAL POINTS

So how do we protect our time? What hacks can we implement to protect ourselves from all of the distractions we endure throughout a typical day? Let's start with what protecting our time is not. It is not ceasing to use social media, cell phones and computers. That would be backwards progress. And that's a solution that's only temporary, at best. These tools can be wonderfully helpful and powerful. I certainly agree with those who think a period of fasting from social media and cell phone use has many benefits. But, when used appropriately, our digital tools can amplify our success. So, instead of leaping to the most extreme conclusions, consider taking small, simple steps to protect our time and make the most out of the opportunities we have before us.

The first step is to manipulate your environment. We've already talked about this in previous chapters but it's worth going through again. Whether at home or in your office, put your toys out of sight. I've noticed that it works for me quite well. The old adage "out of sight out of mind" really resonates with me. If I'm writing or studying and I see my phone sitting there, I am totally tempted to quickly check and see if anyone texted me. It is even more important to hide your screens when spending quality time with a spouse or child. Once our tools have been solidified as habits in our lives, the mere sight of them triggers an unconscious loop that leads quickly to distraction. So, do your family and yourself a huge favor and put your toys out of sight so you can focus on what's really important.

Second, you absolutely have to close your email, messaging and social media applications when doing deep work. I'm going to give you a real example to show you that even I need to follow my own advice. As I'm writing this sentence, this actual sentence that you're reading right now, I received an email and a text. They were from different people, regarding different matters. I diverted to each of them to "get it out of the way so I can focus and write with a clear mind." You know what happened? The sentence above took about twenty-three minutes to write. I'm not exaggerating. The sentence took twenty-three minutes to write because my replies solicited responses from the senders that started another cycle of distractions. My train of thought was totally wrecked. What's funny is that neither message was an emergency and could have easily waited until my next scheduled break. The problem was that I couldn't wait. I saw the little red circle with the number of notifications down at the bottom of my laptop's dock and couldn't stop looking at it. It haunted me, and if the sentences above don't flow, it's because I couldn't concentrate. (You'll probably not ever notice because my editor Rachel rocks, but still, they were probably raw and incoherent.) So, I obliged and looked. Just a quick look. One little second became twenty-three minutes of wasted time.

I'm sure you know exactly what I'm talking about. I'm sure you've faced the very same thing during your busy work day. Imagine if I closed the apps. Imagine if I never saw the red notification circles. Could I have not had a better chance of writing that sentence in twenty-three seconds instead of twenty-three minutes? You know it and I know it. So, close your apps, turn off your notifications and do your work.

Imagine, if you will, the quiet you experience on a six-hour flight from LAX to Maui. You have no signal on your phone. No Wi-Fi, no LTE and no 5G. It's totally quiet. You have no access to anyone and they have no access to you, at least for the six hours you're over the Pacific. You could purchase the inflight Wi-Fi to text with your buddies back home but you really don't want to pay $20 for the Wi-Fi that you'll get for free at the hotel. You're excited about the opportunity to get some work done and take advantage of the solitude. So, you sit quietly and work. My challenge to you today is to make that imaginary flight to Maui something real each and every day. Plus, dude, Maui. You're going to Maui.

Another major cause of sand and gravel filling your jar is something I like to call handing off your to-do list. Handing off your to-do list is something on the verge of an epidemic. I've done it and had others do it to me. What I mean is this, how often has someone sent you an email with something that they needed from you? When you received it, you knew it was something on their to-do list. But if they sent it to you and put it on your to-do list, they got something off their plate and moved closer to inbox zero. I'm sure there's not a one of us who hasn't done that. My poor assistant had to deal with me doing that every day until I figured it out!

And it doesn't end there. Now you feel pressure to respond right away to acknowledge receipt of the email. So, while you should be focused on writing the big report, getting the quarterly financials complete or enjoying a date with your spouse, someone else's to-do list got in your way. Instead of doing your work, focusing on your big rocks, you've taken on a task that another person has thrown at you. This is reason alone to make sure your email inbox and apps are closed while you're trying to work.

What if you were to say no to that email request? Could you do that to a subordinate? To someone you love? To your boss? I've found that most people truly want to serve and help other people and so the immediate default is to say yes to any and every request that comes our way. But this isn't effective and hardly crucifixional. To say yes to every request is ultimately to say no to all of them. As amazing as you are, you're not able to accomplish everything. No one is. If we were really to stop and think about the full consequences of saying yes to a particular request, I think we'd find that we'd be more inclined to say no a lot more often. In fact, I think for us to be truly effective, we have to say no ninety-five percent of the time. Saying no can be a difficult thing to do. Guess what the next chapter is about?

Go get some.

24

SAYING NO

Tim Tassopoulos is the President and COO of Chick-fil-A. At a conference together a few years ago, he told us the story of Dan Cathy's encounter with the Atlanta Falcons. Dan, the CEO and son of Chick-fil-A founder S. Truett Cathy, met with the Falcons as they were building their new multi-billion-dollar home, Mercedes-Benz Stadium. With corporate headquarters in Atlanta and a local staple in that city, it seemed only fitting for the Falcons to offer Chick-fil-A the rights to purchase space in the new stadium's concession level. Flattered, Cathy was glad to accept the space. But he had one small condition. As a committed Christian family and corporation, Chick-fil-A honors the Sabbath. That means they don't open their restaurants on Sundays. If the Falcons were not willing to accept that term, Cathy's answer would be no.

The power of his no might not be clear until you remember that NFL games are played on Sundays. With the Mercedes-Benz stadium able to hold 71,000 fans, that equates to a tremendous amount of lost revenue. When asked why Cathy was able to say no, Tim replied, "Dan said, 'our light shines brightest when our lights are dark.'" Dan Cathy's values and purpose are more important to him than revenue. He was able to stand by his values because he was able to say no.

§ SAYING NO IN CONTEXT

I used to be a people-pleaser. I wanted everyone to be happy and enjoy life. If I could offer anything to help them accomplish that, I was almost always inclined to do so. As I spent more time working in my parish, it began to grow and grow. More and more people came to our church each week. Alongside that growth, the requests from people for my time increased dramatically. There were new ideas to discuss, meetings to attend, baptisms to perform, weddings to celebrate, lunch meetings to host and pastoral care to do. As a people-pleaser who had a hard time saying no, it quickly became overwhelming for any one person to manage, at least effectively.

To put this in perspective, one day I performed a simple exercise. There are 8,760 hours in a year. Twenty-four hours a day multiplied by 365 days a year. If I only sleep five hours a day—clearly far less than necessary—that gives me 6,935 hours per year to accomplish my work and be a successful pastor. Now assume that the only work I do is my Sunday morning worship and preaching—say three hours for each of the fifty-two weeks in a year. That leaves a total of 6,779 hours in the year to do everything.

We have approximately 300 families that we account for in our parish. Accounting for those who are single and those who are married with children, we approximate 1,000 people that I pastorally care for. That means there are 6.8 hours per year to dedicate to each member of my flock. Less than seven hours per year! With that small amount of time, how effective can any one person be? I think you know the answer.

The list above is not realistic, either. In the calculations we only talk about Sunday morning worship. We didn't include spending time with my bride and daughters, exercise, study, funerals, confessions, travel, writing, preparing sermons and bible studies, office management, mentoring my team, driving, hospital ministry, visiting the elderly, spending time with friends and finding quiet time to think and reflect.

So, I ask again, how effective can any one person be? At this pace, not very. In one of my favorite books, *Essentialism*, author Greg McKeown claims that until you learn how to say no, "You will find yourself making a millimeter of progress in a million different directions." Which is to say you are making no progress at all.

The goal of *Essentialism* is to help the reader offer their highest contribution to the world. According to McKeown, there are three key fallacies that prohibit us from doing so. These fallacious thoughts are:

1. I have to;
2. Everything is important;
3. I can do both.

If we're honest with ourselves, we know how accurate his assessment of typical American life is. I firmly believe the stress accompanying our time constraints is a major contributor to the health epidemic we're facing as a nation. So how do we combat that? How do we conquer these three fallacies and offer our highest contribution to the world? McKeown suggests replacing them with the following:

1. I choose to;
2. Very few things are important;
3. I can do anything, but I can't do everything.

Okay, but how do we do that? We do that by using one of the most important words in the English language: no.

Saying no can be one of the most difficult things to say. We want to please people. It makes us happy to help other people. Sometimes we're afraid or uncomfortable to say no when we know we should. It's in our nature not to upset or offend another person. Feeling a sense of obligation is another major culprit in our inability to say no. We feel reciprocity strongly and believe that because someone did something for us, we can't say no to their request. We owe them. It's easy to say yes to every request that comes our way. Though common, submitting to these temptations enables our schedule to manage us rather than us managing our schedule. And it is by no means crucifixional.

Before I began practicing the *Art of No*, my schedule owned me. I ran from meeting to meeting accomplishing very little. I would come home at the end of each day totally exhausted and feeling completely unproductive. I had worked hard to be sure, but I hadn't done very much good work. Sure, I had met with people and listened to their ideas and challenges. But what did I offer them in return? I had committed to being in too many places at the same time. My sense of obligation even forced me to commit to things I wasn't qualified or trained to handle. I was giving very little back to the world. And early one Sunday morning I woke up and couldn't feel half of my face.

§ GOD'S INPUT

We have a responsibility to give our best to the world. And when we're so swamped with appointments, we can't do that. In his Epistle to the Ephesians, St. Paul exhorts us to manage our time well. He says, "Look carefully then how you walk, not as unwise men but as wise, **making the most of the time** for the days are evil," (Eph. 5:15-16, emphasis mine). In the larger context of this verse, St. Paul is asking the Ephesian Christians not to waste their time on superfluous tasks but rather to focus on work that brings light to the world. He recognized that if his Christian community in Ephesus was properly focused on the will of Lord and doing the right things, they wouldn't have time to do all the unnecessary and evil things that pulled at them. But that meant saying no to all of the things that got in the way of making their highest contribution to the world.

§ PRACTICAL POINTS

Now that we understand how important saying no is, how do we implement that in our lives? Are there tools we can implement to help us avoid falling into the three fallacies McKeown exposes? You know it. We offer three practical points to get us on our way: conquer guilt, build a response buffer and get a support team.

First, let's conquer guilt. As we've seen throughout this chapter, saying no can be difficult, especially when we feel guilty for doing so.

Unfortunately, that's what I call a *you* problem. You've just submitted to the fallacy of "I have to". The only one who feels guilt is you. And you have to get over it. You don't have to do everything that comes your way in this life. You have the option to choose what you will and won't commit to. Exercise that option. Others recognize that you're busy, they're busy too! We all know that no person can say yes to every request that comes their way. Sure, they may be disappointed if you decline, but they'll respect you more for it, trust me. Hearing someone brag about how busy their schedule is does not impress me. I actually feel sad for the person knowing the difficulties they must be facing. Instead, recognize that your time is valuable and you need to use it to do good work. No more mediocrity. You owe the world your very best. If you're going to feel guilty, do so for not giving your best.

Next, build a response buffer. Never commit to a request for your time on the spot. Go back to your calendar with a clear mind before committing to anything. When I'm away from my office and someone asks for my time, I simply urge them to send me, or my assistant, an email and I will get back to them. Most importantly, by doing this, the request is now in writing so I won't forget about it. Blowing someone off is not good! Delaying your response also creates a buffer between the sense of obligation felt at that moment and good decision making. When confronted with a request for your time, there is pressure to respond immediately. That immediacy often leads to poor decision making. We usually respond better to any situation the further we're removed from it. That includes our schedule.

The second part of building a response buffer regards email. If you are like the vast majority of people in the world today, emails race to your inbox regularly throughout the day. Whether they include an actual appointment request or not, each and every email requires your time. As we saw from the previous chapter, it only takes six emails to usurp an hour of your time. It is essential that we build a buffer between receiving an email and responding to it. A newfound obligation to respond to each and every email the moment they arrive in our inbox is simply absurd. Why have we put that pressure on ourselves? Feeling obliged to respond immediately is wrong on so many different levels, not the least of which is falling victim to the third fallacy above, which is "I can do both". How can you focus on the important task you're currently working on if you're constantly replying to emails? You can't and you know it.

Build a response buffer. There are a multitude of hacks you could implement but the ones I use seem to work fairly well. First, I don't look at my email until noon. Nothing earth shattering will happen before noon anyhow. And by that time, I've already completed some good focused work. Second, that means the notifications need to be turned off. The notification systems on all of our platforms are habit-forming by design, as we've previously discussed. I am unable to see the notification number in the red circle on my phone or laptop and not engage it. So, I just eliminated those notifications. That means email, Facebook, Instagram, Snapchat, text messages, WhatsApp, LinkedIn, all of them. Turn your notifications off. Lastly, be prepared to reject ninety-five percent of the requests you receive. That's right, ninety-five percent. Obviously that number could vary, but the point should be clear. Just because someone is sending you an email to free up their to-do list doesn't mean it needs to be on yours. If very few things matter—say five percent of your opportunities—then you need to have proper time set aside to focus on them.

The final practical point is to surround yourself with a good support team. If you are blessed with someone working for you, allow them to say no for you. I have the best assistant on the planet. Tisha is efficient, organized and graceful. Recently, I relinquished my calendar to her care with the instructions to protect me from myself. Now, any and every request for my time is sent directly to her. That means when someone asks for my time, I ask them to email or speak to Tisha and she will schedule it as soon as time permits. You cannot get to me without going through her. With a much clearer head and a bird's eye view of my days, weeks and months, she is able to properly place requests for my time on the calendar. Because of that, I'm no longer rushed and can give my very best to each person I spend time with.

Just because you may not have someone working for you doesn't mean a support team can't be built. Stop making excuses and build your support team! Could a spouse or friend help by holding you accountable? Maybe you have to report in at the end of each day? Whatever creative idea you come up with, make sure you have a team to help you.

For many of us, saying no is not an easy habit to establish. The more we begin implementing no into our lives, the easier it becomes. And the better we feel.

Go get some.

25

DO BUSINESS NOT BUSYNESS

Bill Belichick is probably the best head coach the NFL has ever seen. His head coaching statistics are off the chart. He's been voted as Coach of the Year on three separate occasions. He's won an astounding seventy percent of the games he's coached with a career record of 304-137. Thirty-one of those wins were in the postseason. Speaking of the postseason, that's where Belichick kicks into overdrive. His postseason record of 31-12 boasts a seventy-two percent win rate, which is impressive in and of itself. Add that to the fact that nine of those games have been the Super Bowl. That's right, nine Super Bowls. Sadly, he's only won six of those Super Bowls. He holds the records for most Super Bowl appearances, most Super Bowl wins and most playoff wins. Whether you like the New England Patriots or not, you've got to give Belichick his props. He handles business.

What makes Coach Belichick so effective? How is he able to put forth excellence each and every year no matter who his players are or how often they change? What is it about his style that just simply wins, much to the chagrin of the New York Jets? His focus is certainly part of it. If you ever need a good laugh, watch Belichick's post-game interviews with the press. It's so awkward and uncomfortable that one can't help but laugh. He's famous for simple and terse responses to the reporters' questions. Ignoring the reasons his team won or lost on that particular day, he regularly responds to the media in curt tones that he and his team are only focused on the next week's game. That's it. "We're focused on Pittsburgh," or, "We're on to Miami." The next opponent is Belichick's only business. And here's the kicker: anything that isn't about that business is of no value to Belichick. He dismisses it outright and gets back down to business. His business. If what you have to say to him isn't about his business, then he dismisses it as busyness. That right there, the difference between business and busyness, is the distinction Coach Belichick uses to be so successful.

℥ BUSINESS NOT BUSYNESS IN CONTEXT

Busyness is doing non-essential tasks that add little or no value to your overall goal and is a crime that most of us succumb to on a regular basis. I sure did. Daily. Like every single day. I was so easily distractible with whatever came my way that I easily got lost in the busyness of mundane tasks that only seemed to further someone else's business. If something popped up or a notification chimed, it took my entire being to ignore it. It was a vortex that just kept sucking me in deeper and deeper until there was no escape!

All great achievers stress how important their mornings are. You can read just about any efficiency expert and you will hear story after story of how they do their best work in the morning. Even NFL football coaches, Belichick included, are notorious for being in their offices watching film or planning their running attack as early as 4:30 a.m. They get up early and get right down to business before the chaos of the day gets in the way. This is excellent advice. It was advice I wanted to follow, so three years ago, I dedicated myself to a morning routine. To give us an example, let's look at it. My morning routine is scheduled as follows:

> 6:00 a.m. - Wake
> 6:10 a.m. - Prayer
> 6:30 a.m. - Coffee
> 7:00 a.m. - Exercise
> 8:00 a.m. - Shower and dress
> 8:30 a.m. - Write
> 10:30 a.m. - Go to the office for the day

It's pretty straightforward and simple to follow. Unless I open my laptop. Then I'm done. Toast. As soon as I open the laptop, Pandora unleashes her wrath. All of the emails from the past eight hours come flooding in. The Facebook notifications start chiming. There's always a handful of early morning texters. And I haven't even opened ESPN or the news yet. Now none of that is inherently bad in and of itself. It's when I submit to the temptation to get into the busyness that my business doesn't get done.

I like *inbox zero*. That means that because I use my email inbox as a to-do list of sorts, I feel good when it's empty. Reaching inbox zero means I'm all caught up and can now focus on the important business. In theory, that's a great idea. In reality, inbox zero is harder to achieve than hitting the lottery. First, responding to emails is very often not the most essential part of your day. For example, among others sitting in my email inbox at this very moment is an email from myself reminding me to send an email to a parishioner (I wish I was joking). There is another email from a friend asking me to write a review for his forthcoming book, a draft email from my assistant to send the service schedules to our parish and a thank you email from a dear friend. Not one of those can't wait. Not one of those emails is urgent. Not one of those is actually important to my personal goal of teaching crucifixional living to the entire planet. Not one. They're just keeping me busy.

Second, while I'm attacking this particular batch of non-essential emails, something awful happens. New emails start coming in. They're just as unimportant as the first batch of emails but I think, "I'll just bang them out really quick" so I'm free to focus on the real business. But while working on email batch two, the third batch starts trickling in.

You know what I'm talking about. It's an endless cycle. And the worst part of this chaos is that we are actively busy doing other people's work! That's right, other people's work. Coach Belichick is not interested in anyone else's work. He doesn't do busyness. He does business. And wins Super Bowls.

Do you find yourself chasing busyness and not being as productive as you want to be? If so, you've fallen prey to the *Busyness Syndrome*. How many of us are guilty of that? We feel tension because we know God has asked us to contribute our very best to the world. He has commissioned us to be light to the world, to be Warrior Saints, living crucifixionally for the sake of others, for the sake of a greater good and of glory to His name. That is the business we must attend to. We are supposed to do that in every aspect of our lives. But when we get distracted with busyness, however, our focus is diverted from our real purpose and flits about from desire to desire. There is an old saying of unknown origin that says, "If you chase two rabbits, both will escape". That is to say, if we are lost in the mundane of busyness, the success of our business has no chance.

♪ GOD'S INPUT

Jesus has made it fairly clear to us that not everything is of equal importance. Furthermore, while we don't disparage the more mundane tasks of life that have to be done, the best part of our effort needs to be directed towards Him and living a crucifixional life. This is perhaps best illustrated for us in a story about Mary and Martha. Luke 10:38-42 tells us that as Jesus was journeying, He entered a village where two sisters lived. These sisters, Mary and Martha, invited the Lord into their home to share a meal and to spend some time with Him. Because a great teacher was coming to her home, Martha was busy preparing and serving everything. I imagine she was preparing food and drink, getting utensils to serve, dishes, cups and all the things needed to entertain a visitor of great stature. Her sister Mary, however, contented herself to sit at the Lord's feet and listen to His teaching. The image here is one of a student sitting at the feet of a great master to hear His words and learn wisdom needed for an upright life. As this could have possibly been their lone encounter with Jesus, Mary wasn't going to squander her opportunity to get down to the real business.

Martha, however, was irritated that her sister left her to do all the busywork by herself. And what every person consumed with busyness does, she complained about it and asked Jesus to tell her sister to help. His response was unexpected and sharp. "Martha, Martha, you are anxious and troubled about many things; one thing is needful. Mary has chosen the good portion, which shall not be taken away from her," (Luke 10:41-2). The power of His statement is that only one thing really matters, His teaching, which is the good portion. Serving guests is nice, but the real business is hearing His teaching. And because Mary recognized that and rejected all the mundane busyness, she would not lose her reward.

There is a powerful lesson in the story of these two sisters. While busywork does need to happen, it cannot be at the expense of the real business of our lives. Busyness must be set aside to focus on God and His word and then to do it. This relentless elimination of all things mundane is crucifixional living *par excellence*.

℥ PRACTICAL POINTS

Since we're talking about our work lives, can this idea apply to the business of our business also? You bet it can! We began this chapter with Coach Bill Belichick and his ruthless elimination of anything distracting him from his mission. It seems appropriate, therefore, to glean our first practical point from him. It is said that when it comes to football, Belichick lives by one maxim from *The Art of War* by Chinese military strategist Sun Tzu. The saying is, "Every battle is won before it is fought." Though we're not talking about war with another nation, the message is crystal clear: be prepared. You can imagine the countless hours Belichick spends watching his opponents' game film. The time he spends drawing up game plans, the practices he meticulously puts his players through, learning the referees' habits, studying the rules of the game and so on. Other NFL franchises, coaches and commentators marvel how Belichick's team is always more prepared than anyone they play against. The other team may be more physically gifted, but they will never be more prepared than the New England Patriots.

To apply this to our own work means that we have to spend some serious time in preparation. No matter what your business is, you can never be too prepared. There are some concepts to consider in that regard. Have you created a goal that you want to attain this month and made a plan to achieve it? What are the actionable steps you intend to take today, this week, this month to reach that goal? Can you imagine some obstacles that you will encounter along the way as you try to implement your plan? Who are you trusting to contribute to the overall success of your vision and plan? What emergencies may arise that you are not envisioning? Is your budget allocated properly? There are countless questions you must ask yourself if you want to be properly prepared to face the challenges of running a successful business.

A key component of preparation is implementing a plan to remove the distractions that you know are inevitably coming. Using my morning example above, the only way for me to stay on course is outsmart my laptop. Before I go to sleep, I close my email application and my browser. It seems silly at first, but by doing this, I know that if I am tempted to open my laptop before my prayer and exercise are completed, at least the notifications and triggers won't be visible. It's a simple example, sure, but it should make the necessity of preparation crystal clear.

The second practical point is to use a tool that helps establish what is really important. Oftentimes, we get lost in busyness because we haven't clearly delineated what the important things are that we have to accomplish today. There are a lot of helpful tools out there to get to keep us on track. I personally like the Eisenhower Matrix. The Eisenhower Matrix is a simple square with four smaller squares inside it. The top left box is for tasks that are important and urgent. The top right box is for tasks that are important but not urgent. The bottom left box is for unimportant and urgent tasks while the last box is for the unimportant and not urgent.

THE EISENHOWER MATRIX

	URGENT	NOT URGENT
IMPORTANT	**DO IT FIRST**	**SCHEDULE IT**
NOT IMPORTANT	**DELEGATE IT**	**DELETE IT**

In the graphic, you can clearly see the order in which you should approach your daily tasks and if you should even approach some tasks at all. The real business needs to be done first. Delegate urgent tasks that are unimportant. If it matters and can wait, schedule it for later in the day. And my favorite square is to altogether eliminate the busyness that is neither urgent nor important. You may find a tool you like better than the Eisenhower Matrix, but I encourage you to make it a daily habit of using something that will help you stay focused on the real business at hand. Once you find one you like, you must stay committed to using it. Fight the temptation to ignore it, if even just for one day. Doing that is how we found ourselves victims to the *Busyness Syndrome* in the first place!

Finally, our third practical is point is to stop doing other people's work. Doing tasks for other people is a time-suck that doesn't further your own business. Our inclination is to help others when asked, and

I encourage that strongly. But just because something mundane is on your to-do list doesn't mean that it needs to be on mine. How often have we received an email where a colleague or co-worker throws a request at us that we know is just clearing up clutter on their desk? Kudos to them for trying to stay efficient, but we have a duty to accomplish our goals and tasks first. Remember, you have been called by God to offer your best to the world. How can you give your best if you're constantly busy with the tasks of others? It is imperative that you learn the art of the graceful no. Saying no is often so difficult that we dedicated an entire chapter of this book to it. I encourage you to read that chapter again if you haven't already.

Go get some.

26

CONTROL

Recently, someone in my parish didn't like a policy I implemented and called me a control junkie. As I thought about those words, I wondered if wanting control was actually a bad thing. To be sure, when someone calls you this it is probably intended as an insult of sorts or to try to keep you in check. But is wanting to be in control really a bad thing? Can you be a control seeker and produce good results? An even bigger question is can you seek to be in control and still trust in God? Let's explore these questions.

A quick Google search doesn't reveal a lot of positive statements about being someone seeking control. Most articles on the internet speak about this in a negative light. Some of these articles go so far as to accuse these people of suffering from Obsessive Compulsive Disorder and Anxiety. It seems to me, however, that people use the moniker as an insult to make the recipient feel bad. Or, perhaps to intimidate him into behaving in a desired way. Even more so, people accuse others of control seeking because they actually feel out of control in their own lives. They seem to find balance when others appear as out of control as they do themselves.

So, let's start asking tougher questions. Is wanting to take control a bad thing? If we attempt to control other people's lives, thoughts and survival then indeed, it can be a bad thing. I am thinking here about extremes, however. The Soviet gulags or Nazi concentration camps of the mid-20th century come to mind. But is that what the detractor means when he calls you names? I'm not so sure.

For example, over the past twenty-plus years I have been working hard to build a thriving and healthy parish. And as I write this, we're also working very hard to build a successful Warrior Saints Movement. Both of these endeavors are incredibly important to me and to countless others. Should I leave the success of these two ministries to chance? Should I cross my fingers and hope they work out well? Or, as the leader who bears the responsibility for their success, shouldn't I take total control of all the plans, actions and outcomes? I'm sure by now you know the answer. As the leader, it is my responsibility to take as much control of every single aspect of a successful outcome as I possibly can and to guide and influence my team towards achieving our goals. It's my responsibility to make sure the things we need to have happen actually happen.

℘ CONTROL IN CONTEXT

My response to the person in my parish who attempted to insult me by calling me names was, "Yeah, I am! I am a control junkie and freely admit it." I'd rather maintain control than relinquish it to someone else.

Because we know that every good leader feels responsibility to take control of the outcome of his goals and mission, what would compel someone to use this moniker as an insult? I believe people say this because they feel no power over the outcomes of their life and they are thirsting to be in control! This disharmony between internal feelings and external environment often lead to moments of anxiety. So rather than taking charge of positive outcomes in their own lives, these people often default into creating a chaos outside themselves to match the chaos they feel inside. Rather than do the hard work to improve themselves and their environment, they attack others who are moving forward. This is an attempt to bring balance to the chaos experienced in their life. "My life is a mess and I will feel better when everyone else's life is a mess too!"

Knowing that, it is for Warrior Saints to be crucifixional. We must be compassionate, understand the anxiety that person may be experiencing and move forward with love and gentility. It is as simple as smiling to a person, accept the sobriquet as a compliment and continue moving forward within control to accomplish your goals.

§ GOD'S INPUT

Now we ask the hardest question: can I be a control seeker and still trust in God? Are the two mutually exclusive? If I'm trying to take control of my time, my environment, my systems and my actions, is there room for me to still trust in God? Or should I just step back and hope that God will accomplish the things on my behalf that I've set out to do?

I want to revisit a verse we used earlier in our chapter "Courage." The Prophet Isaiah gives us some great insight on how to take action while always trusting in God. In chapter 41 we hear, "For I, the LORD your God hold your right hand; it is I who say to you, 'Fear not, I will help you,'" (Is. 41:13). This verse is awesome! In it, we hear God saying, "Don't be afraid, I got you! I will help you through the tough times." Holding our right hand is not to be thought of literally as though God is holding our hand and walking along with us until two sets of footprints become one, as discussed earlier. What Isaiah means is that God is with us, therefore, trust Him. "Trust in the way that I have taught you. Trust in the teachings I have given you. Trust that if you follow My instructions and live your life in the manner in which I have shown you to live, it will go well with you." Simply put? Trust in the crucifixional lifestyle.

Let's consider a simple hypothetical example. Imagine that you are in high school and have a big chemistry test tomorrow. It's an important test because it will influence your GPA and, therefore, the university that you will attend. This test really matters and you want to nail it. In your unflinching trust in the Lord you pray, "O God, I am going to trust in you that tomorrow you will shine your light down upon me and help me get an *A* on this exam." How do you think that's going to end? With God sending a magic burst of chemistry knowledge into your head? Like Morpheus uploading a judo app into Neo's brain? Come on man, you and I both know it doesn't work like that. If you don't study, you're going to fail. You know it. And I know it, too. I had to learn that one the hard way.

To trust in God actually means something very different. It means that we trust in His word and we trust in His way. To trust in God means that we are willing to accept that His way of crucifixional living is the only way to be successful. We trust that His way of living a sacrificial life is the only way that works. To trust God means that we trust in what He says. And we do it. I'm not looking for God to do my work for me, I'm looking to follow the way that He shows me. So, what do I do? I turn off Monday Night Football, put my phone on silent and study. Now I have a chance for the *A* that I'm looking for.

℥ PRACTICAL POINTS

So how do I take control of the outcomes of my goals? We have four practical points to help us. First, take control of your environment. There are a lot of distractions we encounter on a daily basis. A Netflix binge, getting lost on TikTok, checking on your Fantasy Football team, Snapping with your friends, surfing Facebook and Instagram, watching Game of Thrones or Ozark. Whatever it may be, there are a lot of distractions out there. To be successful, we're going to have to take control of our environment and remove those distractions. Put the phone down, close the laptop and hide your iPad. The tools that are designed to make our lives easier can easily make them more challenging. So put the toys away.

It's also important to be in a place that isn't connected to your distractions. Certainly, going to a library can be helpful, but be cautious of coffee shops. There are always lots of interesting people in a coffee shop to distract us! If you are at home or in your office, find a new place that is specific to study or prep work. Stay clear of the locations that are most connected to your distractions. For example, in my home, I like to end my day with a nice single malt, a cigar and perhaps a Lakers game on the outside patio. With the blessings of living in Arizona, I have about 350 nights a year that I can sit out there and unwind. It has become a place of solitude and recharge for me. Because of this, it is also a place of distraction. Very rarely can I sit on my patio and get real work done. The temptation is to light a stick and turn on the TV. I've lost before I've even started. Instead, I have allocated new space in my home that is distinct to doing work. I don't hang out in this room, I don't watch TV in this room, I don't sleep in this room. I just work in this room. It has been tremendously helpful for me.

Practical point number two is to control your time and your schedule. This is perhaps one of the most important things to finding success in 21st century North America and yet one of the most neglected. There are numerous chapters in this book dedicated to helping you do that very thing. But for our purposes here, remember that it is important to be mindful about what you schedule. You cannot say yes to every opportunity or request that comes across your inbox. No one on the planet has enough time to say yes to all of the requests we receive and still be successful. And yet we constantly convince ourselves that we can. And we say yes.

Instead, say yes to only the top five percent of requests you get. Ask yourself, will this help me get ahead? If I say yes to this opportunity, will it help me accomplish my goals? If the answer to those questions is not a resounding yes, then you should probably skip it. Entrepreneur and author Derek Sivers says it best: "No more 'yes'" when teaching how to emphatically commit to something.[14]

Our third practical point is to take control of yourself. One of the hardest things for leaders who are control seekers to do is get out of his team's way. But if we've built the right team with the right people in the right places and given clear goals, instructions and expectations, it is our job to get out of their way and turn them loose to do their job. We've

---

[14] https://sivers.org/hellyeah

got to be crucifixional and sacrifice our own desire to micromanage our people—remember controlling other people can be bad—and allow the experts to do what they do best. We'll learn more about this in the next chapter.

Lastly, we have to control who we spend our time with. Again, that does not mean that we control other people. It means that we have to take control of the people that we allow ourselves to spend time with. If you put a sponge in a bucket of water, it is going to absorb the water. It has no other choice than to do so. A sponge in water will get wet. You and I are kind of like sponges too. And if we imagine that the bucket of water is the world we inhabit, our environment, it should stand to reason to make sure that our bucket is filled with clear water. The people we interact with are like the water. There are people who are really good to be around and there are some who we are probably better off avoiding. We all know that guy or gal who is toxic to be around. We all know a person who is doing things that don't line up with our morals, values and goals. We all know the guy who is just simply miserable and rotten all the time. And just as a sponge cannot help but absorb water in the bucket, so too do we absorb the toxicity and actions of those we spend our time with.

Instead, we have to control who we spend our time with. If you put yourself in the right circles, you will often find the people you spend your time with can be better than you! That's exactly what we want to have happen. You always want to spend time with people who are better than you. You want people who are going to push you, stretch you and help you grow. You don't want to waste your precious moments with angry, broken people who only want to bring you down. You want to constantly be pushed to become the very best version of yourself that you can possibly be. So, make sure the water in your bucket is crystal clear.

Go get some.

27

CONTROL ON A TEAM

In the previous chapter we discovered that it's okay to be accused of seeking control. We also learned that we can trust in God and still look for control. The key is to trust that His way works and then take control of our actions ourselves to make our goals happen. In this chapter, we're going to see if it's possible to maintain control while working on a team.

The parish I serve was assigned to host a conference in July 2016 for all of the local churches in our geographical region. It was an exciting time for us. We began preparations nearly four years in advance which meant the organizational and administrative tasks had to be flawless. The conference would have a ton of moving parts and any hiccups could prove disastrous. Managing that kind of detail is beyond my comfort zone and skill set, so I asked some incredible people from the parish to lead our conference team. As the pastor of the parish, I certainly had authority to veto any decisions, but I had the best possible leaders in place. So, I decided to make myself a part of the team and defer to their leadership. Together with those committee heads, we selected a small group of stellar individuals to comprise the leadership team for the conference. We were off and running!

As every project of this magnitude encounters challenges, ours was no different. The diocese that we belong to has a committee that is tasked with oversight of all conferences and we would be working with them. This particular committee, located in another state, has been known to be control monsters. And not in the positive sense described in the previous chapter. Because they wanted to make every decision for our conference, it became clear there would be tension for the next four years. They had such negative control issues that our team was not sure why they even needed us to plan the conference! Keep this fact in the back of your minds for the time being.

℘ CONTROL ON A TEAM IN CONTEXT

Seeking control and working on a team can produce one of two outcomes. The first is not so much fun. When someone working with a team tries to make every decision, take every action and handle every job, it is inevitably an unpleasant experience for everyone involved. If that person is going to do all of the work and make all of the decisions for the team, why does he even need a team in the first place? Seriously, just do the work yourself and let the rest of us avoid the headaches! If the committee from the diocese wanted to plan everything, they should have just planned everything. Why even ask us to get involved? We were doing quite well without the project!

The second possible outcome is saturated with potential success. The leader, who bears ultimate responsibility for the project, should put a team in place, give clear direction, set clear expectations and goals and then gets out of the way. Turn your team loose to do what they do best. If the leader has done his job properly, he has placed the right people on the team and in the right spot on the team. If he has done it correctly, every position is handled by the expert in that field and the leader can focus on what he is supposed to be doing. He must be a part of the team, to be sure, but strong enough to defer to those whom he has placed in charge. Otherwise, as we've already noted, just do the work all by yourself and save the rest of us from your headaches.

ᶘ GOD'S INPUT

In 1 Corinthians, the Apostle Paul uses the metaphor of the body to make this very point. Speaking to a community that appears to have been suffering from in-fighting, he shows that the human body has many different parts, each with a specific task and function. "For the body does not consist of one member but of many . . . If all were a single organ, where would the body be? As it is, there are many parts yet one body. The eye cannot say to the hand, 'I have no need of you,' nor again the head to the feet, 'I have no need of you,'" (1 Cor. 12:14, 19-21).

In this elegant chapter, St. Paul is telling his community that they must work together as a team. Each person on the team has a specific function to perform. No part is less important than another, but all work together in harmony. There is certainly a head to this body, but the eyes do the seeing and the ears do the hearing and the feet do the walking, and so on. Each part of the body does what it's supposed to do. Understanding this is when you find success.

ᶘ PRACTICAL POINTS

So can a control seeker work positively on a team? Of course. How about some practical points on the Way of the Warrior Saint that you can implement immediately?

First, when building a team, you must put the right people in place. You have to make the right decision when you hire someone. You have to make the right decision when you select a volunteer. I cannot stress this enough. If you accept the wrong person for a position out of fear or obligation, you are destined for a world of headache. Ask any business owner and they'll tell you that their main source of headaches come from people. It's because they have the wrong people in place.

In the business classic, *Good to Great*, researcher Jim Collins describes a successful business with the metaphor of a bus. This bus is successful only when all of the people on board are the right people.

This can often be challenging, especially in volunteer situations, but the leader has to be strong enough to enforce it. That means you cannot be afraid to wait for the right person to come along. Just because you are in need of an employee or volunteer doesn't mean you fill a seat on the bus with the first person that comes along. If that person isn't the right fit, be patient and wait for your home-run hitter to show up. That may require you to do their work for a time, but you're a control seeker anyway!

And it doesn't end there, the best bus is the one that also has the right people in the right seats on the bus. Once you've got a team of rock stars in place, you have to give them the jobs for which they are best suited. Let them play to their strengths. As noted above, managing minute detail is not my strong suit and way out of my comfort zone. So, in our 2016 conference, our committee chairs gave the detail and scheduling work to someone more suited for it. She crushed it.

Practical point number two is that once you have the right people in place, the leader must set very clear expectations and goals for them. You can never be too clear. It is unfair for a leader to expect that his employees will draw every line and every conclusion the way they are in your head. We cannot assume our people will understand exactly what we mean. I've come to understand that people interpret the words we say based on their previous experience, understanding and make up. I know we have great trust in our team, but no one is a mind reader. If you want them to know exactly what you expect from them, you must tell them.

Here is a funny example, but one that shows how powerful clarity can be. Let's say I'm in the mood for some chewing gum. I'm reminiscing about my youth and I want some Big League Chew. You know, the kind in the pouch that's cut up to look like the tobacco baseball players fill their cheeks with in the dugout. And I want grape flavor. If I say to my team member, "Can you please get me some gum," how in the world would she have any idea that I want Big League Chew in the pouch that's grape flavor? And if she comes back with Juicy Fruit, could I reasonably be upset with her? Propriety tells me I cannot. Instead, what if I said to her, "I'm in the mood for some chewing gum. Can you please get me grape flavored Big League Chew in the pouch, and don't spend more than $1 and be back here in thirty minutes?" Her goals and expectations are crystal clear. She's happy and I'm happy.

The third practical point is that you must stay connected. Just because you've got the right people in place and given clear instructions doesn't mean you can vanish. Trusting in your team doesn't mean you abandon your team. You're still a part of the team and you have to be with them. Even the best team members still need their leaders. They want your presence, your guidance and support. Remember, you're not doing the work for them, but you're connected for encouragement and questioning and challenging.

The last practical point is that the leader's job is to remove any distraction or obstacle that prevents the team from accomplishing their assigned goals. You should be like a bulldozer that clears everything out of their way so they can succeed. In our earlier example of the 2016 conference, I had the right team in place. And because we had chairs on the committee, I deferred to the decisions they made for the conference. We did what they said, not what I said, even though I'm the pastor of the church and the leader of the team. I had given them the job to lead, so I let them lead. My job was to clear everything else out of their way so they could do that. That meant I was the one to deal with the whiny committee from the diocese. I fielded all of their calls, emails and complaints. I negotiated contracts and schedules. My job was to handle all things mundane so my team could focus on planning a successful conference. My job as the control seeker on the team was to control their environment so that they could succeed. And you know what they did? They planned the most successful conference in our diocese's history.

Seeking control while on a team can be a positive thing. Remember from our practical points to put the right people on your team. You want the very best working with you. Then put them in the right places on the team. Let the experts work on their area of expertise. And don't be afraid to defer to them. If you put them in charge, then they are in charge, even of you! Make certain the goals and expectations are crystal clear. Stay connected as their guide. Lastly, keep all of the distractions out of their way and turn them loose to do what they do best. I promise you, if you maintain control on a team in this way, you will succeed far more than you could ever imagine.

Go get some.

28

MEN OF ACTION

Any discussion about a man of action begins with the 26th President of the United States of America. Born in 1858, Theodore Roosevelt was a sickly child who suffered from debilitating asthma. For most people of his era, asthma would have meant a soft and short life. But not for Roosevelt. Overcoming his sickliness by what he called "living the strenuous life", President Roosevelt exemplified what it means to be a man of action.

His biography is an endless tale of accomplishment after accomplishment. Let's look at some of the most interesting ones. After overcoming his asthma through a strenuous, self-imposed exercise regimen, young Teddy was overpowered in a schoolyard brawl by two older boys. Not content to lose another fight, he found a coach to teach him the art of boxing. He received higher education at Harvard College and attended law school at Columbia. Bored with law, he spent much of that time writing a book about the War of 1812. He served in the New York State assembly from 1882-1884 while also investing in a ranch in the Dakotas where he spent much of the next four years hunting bison and raising cattle. It wasn't until a particularly brutal winter in 1887 wiped out much of his herd that he returned to his home in New York. In 1894, he was appointed to the New York City Board of Police Commissioners and eventually became its president.

Then his life became really interesting. With the Spanish American War beginning in April 1898, Roosevelt resigned from his post as the Assistant Secretary of the Navy and formed the First US Volunteer Cavalry Regiment. Belonging to this new regiment, known as the Rough Riders, was a highly sought-after position. Under his leadership, the Rough Riders found fame during their charge up Kettle Hill and eventually captured it at the cost of over 200 lives. Roosevelt led the charge himself.

His political career is filled with stories too numerous to discuss here, but his life of action did not end after his time as US President. In October 1912, while on the campaign trail, Roosevelt was shot just before delivering a scheduled speech. Luckily, the bullet pierced his glasses case and a folded copy of his speech. Because of that, it did not penetrate all the way into his lung. Normal people would race to the hospital. But not the Bull Moose. Instead, he delivered the speech and fielded questions for ninety minutes! That bullet would remain embedded in his chest for the remainder of his life.

Finally, in 1913-14, Roosevelt joined an expedition in South America that was searching and tracing the headwaters of the Rio da Duvida up to the Amazon River. At one point during his travels, he attempted to leap into the river and he badly cut his leg. The resulting wound became infected and led to an extreme tropical fever. On more than one occasion, Roosevelt begged the expedition to leave him enough morphine for an overdose and carry on without him. His son, Kermit, would not leave him behind, and Roosevelt eventually completed the journey and returned home to New York. The life of this remarkable man is one that all aspiring men of action should become familiar with.

℘ MEN OF ACTION IN CONTEXT

It may not be possible for every one of us to live a life as remarkable as President Roosevelt. However, it does not mean that we cannot become men of action. Though there are many traits for these warriors of action, one thing all men of action have in common is the unwillingness to sit on the sidelines and watch life unfold. They see problems and challenges and spring into action. They do not permit themselves to make excuses and they take responsibility for every outcome in their lives.

In 2005, my bride, my daughter and I went to Columbus, Ohio, to visit my sister, her husband and my newborn nephew. One afternoon we decided as a family to go out for lunch. My sister had one of those double strollers in which two kids can be held in tandem. Upon arriving at the restaurant, we pulled into a parking space along the curb, placed the stroller behind the car and loaded the two kids in it. They were really cute.

With the kids in the stroller below the curb, we gathered our things from the car to go into the restaurant for lunch. Before I realized what was happening, another driver was trying to park his car right behind us. As he was backing into the spot, his trajectory had him pointing right at the stroller. The driver couldn't see it and had no idea that he was about to smash into our children. It was a simple task to stop the impending accident; I could have moved the stroller, knocked on his trunk or simply shouted for him to stop. Instead, I froze. I saw what was about to happen and the fear and devastation of losing the two children threw me into inaction. I literally froze. As I watched, the proverbial life flashed before my eyes.

Thank the good Lord my brother-in-law Waleed is a man of action and simply picked up the stroller and put it on the curb right before the guy ran into our kids. It was a simple action, but it taught me a tremendous lesson that day. Those of us who stand on the sidelines and do nothing are going to have very little success in life. He acted when I froze. That day I was not a man of action. But it was also the last day I stood on the sidelines.

Today, men of action are hard to find. Men certainly want to do well—we want to do great—but often submit to a fear that leads to inaction. It's much easier to sit on the sidelines where it's safe and comfortable. Ignoring our fears or blaming the world for our misfortunes, we become spectators in the game of life. That may seem fun for a while, but inaction prevents us from finding the greatness we're seeking. And worse, inaction can sometimes lead to tragic outcomes for men who sit by comfortably watching life unfold. I was just such a man all those years ago in Columbus, Ohio, watching my children almost get run over by a car.

₷ GOD'S INPUT

One of the most well-known Biblical characters is a man of action named Samson. In the Book of Judges, Samson is described as very strong and adventurous. He rips apart the jaws of lions and wreaks havoc on the enemies of God's people (Judges 13-16).

Those familiar with the story remember his love affair with a wicked woman named Delilah. Delilah, a temptress, hoped to persuade Samson to reveal the source of his strength so that he could be captured and killed by her people, the Philistines. Eventually, Samson fell for her deception and gave away his secret, which was that he had never cut his hair. So late one night, Delilah shaved his head, leaving him weak and vulnerable. The Philistines captured Samson and threw him in prison. He was forced to play the fool at all the fancy Philistine parties. As the story continues, however, something interesting happens. Samson's hair started to grow back and with it came his strength.

The story reaches its climax when Samson called upon the Lord to give him strength once more. If God would restore his strength, he promised to tear down the walls of the house of wickedness. God heeded his call and restored Samson's strength. On his final night, during a party when all of the Philistine lords and ladies were gathered in one place, he toppled the load-bearing pillars of the house and the walls came tumbling down, crushing all of the wicked Philistines.

There's a lot that can be said about the Samson story. Rich in meaning and metaphor, the part that has always stood out in my mind is that Samson was a man of action. He never sat around idly. Constantly causing mischief for the enemies of God's people, Samson did not allow his fear or misfortune to define his life. He went from adventure to adventure as a man of action.

ſ PRACTICAL POINTS

Becoming a man of action can be difficult for some. Like watching your children almost get struck by a car, fear can debilitate the best of us. But men of action learn to conquer their fears. And they never make excuses for the outcomes of their lives. How do men of action do that? Simple. They just start.

Remember, fear can be debilitating. Your battle is to overcome the freeze reaction and spring into action. Maybe you're thinking about writing a book, but you think about how daunting 70,000 words could be. Maybe you'd love to run a marathon, but are stressing out about twenty-six miles. Maybe your wife wants you to fix the back deck but you're not interested in the amount of work it will take. Or maybe you have the desire to level-up in your job or career, but you have to learn a new skill or you have to pass a series test and are afraid you might fail. If you feel any of these fears or others like it, you're certainly not alone. In fact, you're like most people. We all have fear. Our responsibility as Warrior Saints is to be crucifixional and face those fears. So, chart your course and just start.

Writing a book can be scary. Trust me, putting your thoughts out there exposes you to humiliation and mockery. Writing 70,000 words is no simple feat either. But what if you just started with a target of writing 400 words today? That's it. Just write 400 words today. That equates to about a page and a half double spaced. You can do that. And, I'll even bet you find something interesting happen next. As you're writing those 400 words, your mind starts racing and the juices start flowing and before you know it, those 400 words become 1000 words or maybe 2000 words. Think about it like this. A standard book is comprised of around 70,000 words. Do the math. If you end up writing 2000 words a day, in just over one month you've got yourself a book.

Running a marathon is the mark of a man of action. It requires a tremendous amount of time for training and planning. No one just wakes up one day and runs 26.2 miles. It takes a lot of work to train your body to cover that kind of distance. Instead of making excuses that you could never do that, just start today with one mile. Get out of bed and run a mile. Maybe it takes you fifteen minutes. But, so what!

You've started! And I bet that after running one mile every day this week, you'll be ready for two miles a day next week.

Maybe the goal isn't the full twenty-six miles but rather to be committed to regular exercise and optimal health. So what if you're out of shape today! Just start. I have never woken up and said, "Oh man, I can't wait to run!" Running isn't fun for me. And it hurts. It's warmer in bed snuggled under the covers than it is out in the cold morning air. But Warrior Saints confront the discomfort and excuses and just start. Again, I have never regretted running. I have often regretted not running, but I have never regretted running. In the midst of the run, I recognize what I'm doing for my body, for my mind and for those in my life. Don't wait for inspirational music or a nice speech on YouTube from some motivational speaker to kick you into action. Just start. Inspiration rarely leads to sustained action. The converse is equally as true—action often leads to inspiration. If I waited for the moment to feel like running, I wouldn't run very often. If I just start, by the time I get to 0.3 mile, my blood is flowing, and I'm going to run the fastest five miles of my life.

You know that backyard project your wife has been nagging you to complete? What are you waiting for? Wouldn't it be great to have the deck finished so your family could sit outside and enjoy the cool summer evenings? There are no excuses for the amount of work it will require, so just get started. What if you were to start simply by pulling up three planks of the old deck? Would you quit at three planks or would you rip them all out? By starting with three, you're in the groove and the next thing you know, three planks become six planks. Six planks become twelve planks, and before you know it, the old deck is gone. Now you want to go to Home Depot. A veritable playground for the man of action, Home Depot has aisle after aisle of toys and goodies. And soon, you start to find some inspiration. You're asking the experts for some guidance, buying the supplies you need and thinking about those cool summer evenings on the deck with your family. Remember, action leads to inspiration, not the other way around. The key to becoming a man of action is simple: just start!

Go get some.

29

REPETITION

I n the 1996 NBA draft, the Charlotte Hornets selected Kobe Bryant
with the thirteenth overall pick. Because they already had some solid
guards on their team, the Hornets proceeded to trade the rights to Kobe
Bryant to the Los Angeles Lakers in exchange for a center, Vlade Divac.
At the time, it was unclear who got the better end of the deal that day
in June. Knowing what we know now, it's clear that the Lakers got the
better end of the bargain. Divac had a nice career to be sure, but Kobe
is widely considered as one of the best to ever play the game, winning
five NBA championships along with numerous accolades and awards.

Perhaps the most important part of that day was not the draft order
nor the trades nor the championships that would be won. The most
impressive thing is what Kobe did immediately after he was drafted.
According to confidantes of NBA stars, the post-draft tradition is that
after the event, the young men drafted in the first round go out with
their family and friends to celebrate the future with a steak dinner. The
prospect of playing at the most elite level, earning millions of dollars
and becoming a household name is a dream worth celebrating in the
life of those young men. Countless hours and focus went into getting
to that level. There is probably no greater reward than that steak dinner
for the newly drafted. Except Kobe didn't go to dinner. Instead he went
to the gym to practice free throws. You read that right. Kobe didn't go

out to celebrate, he went straight to the gym to shoot free throws. His desire was to be the greatest basketball player in history, so he went to work on that dream immediately.

The helicopter crash in early 2020 that took the life of nine people, including Kobe Bryant and his thirteen-year-old daughter Gianna, put a world-wide spotlight on his accomplishments. The general public has become much more familiar with the success he had over his twenty-year career with the Lakers. The funeral tributes to his victories, scoring titles, All-Star nods and MVP awards were awesome and inspiring to watch. What we didn't see, however, was all the work he did, the sweat he lost and the blood he gave behind the scenes to become the superstar that he was. We didn't see him practice the same drills and moves over and over and over. What we didn't see was the repetition.

ʕ REPETITION IN CONTEXT

Remember our Arabic saying from the chapter "Being Comfortable Being Uncomfortable" that "repetition taught the donkey"? To be a master of any craft requires that we are men and women of repetition. You can be physically and mentally blessed with many gifts and skills, but they will never take you to the highest level on their own. Unless you practice over and over again, the full extent of your talent will never truly be seen. Clearly Kobe had excellent physical skills. He was drafted in the first round of a loaded NBA draft class straight out of high school. But to become the great that he was, he left draft night, went straight to the gym and shot free throw after free throw. His skills made him really good. His repetition made him great.

Doing things over and over again can be cumbersome and perhaps even boring. Performing monotonous tasks *ad infinitum* stretches the limits of human patience. We like trying new things and finding the excitement in a novel concept or idea. Novelty is a powerful driver in the human psyche, so having to repeat the same task seems okay at first, but after a period of time, it becomes difficult to find the inspiration to continue. It's in those moments when we can fall victim to chasing each and every shiny new thing that crosses our path. But chasing the shiny actually takes us further and further away from success. We might become moderately adept at a multitude of tasks but will be exceptional at none of them. Getting better at something, creating new habits and routines, building our gut responses and instincts all take time and repetition.

We've already talked about the maxim attributed to Aristotle, "We are what we repeatedly do. Excellence, then, is not an act, but a habit." I really do love this saying. The great philosopher recognized thousands of years ago exactly what many of us struggle with today. If we want to excel at anything, we have to practice. Over and over again.

Think that's wrong? Remember Allen Iverson? He was a phenomenal player drafted out of Georgetown by the Philadelphia 76ers. Known for his scoring prowess, Iverson was a difficult player to defend. Possibly his most infamous moment, however, came not on the court, but in the interview room. Frustrated when a reporter[15] questioned his dedication to practice, he went on a verbal rampage about the absurdity of the concern and said, "We sitting in here—I'm supposed to be the franchise player—and we in here talking about practice. I mean, listen: We talking about practice. Not a game. Not a game. Not a game. We talking about practice. Not a game. Not the game that I go out there and die for and play every game like it's my last. Not the game. We talking about practice, man." This now famous exchange will be one of the most remembered press conferences for years to come. Iverson was ultimately saying that performing in the game is all that mattered. And to some extent, I agree with him. But it's the repetition beforehand that makes one great in game time situations wherein he and I disagree. Keep in mind, Iverson, who was drafted first overall in the same 1996 draft as Kobe, never won an NBA championship. In fact, he only went to one NBA Finals series in 2001 and lost in five games. Bryant, on the other hand, went to the Finals seven different times and won on five separate occasions, one of which was the 2001 Finals against Iverson's 76ers. Repetition, it seems, definitely makes a difference.

---

[15] https://www.youtube.com/watch?v=eGDBR2L5kzI

ʃ GOD'S INPUT

The Apostle Paul seemed to think so as well. In a letter addressed to his spiritual son Timothy, Paul exhorted his protégé to be a good preacher and teacher to the community that he was leading. Though he was young, Timothy should not have let anyone hold that against him. He was gifted with many skills and needed to work hard to master them. In 1 Timothy, St. Paul writes:

"Let no one despise your youth, but set the believers an example in speech and conduct, in love, in faith, in purity. Till I come, attend to the public reading of scripture, to preaching, to teaching. Do not neglect the gift you have, which was given you by prophetic utterance when the council of elders laid their hands upon you. **Practice these duties, devote yourself to them**, so that all may see your progress. Take heed to yourself and to your teaching; hold to that, for by so doing you will save both yourself and your hearers," (1 Tim. 4:12-16, emphasis mine).

In this passage we hear Paul encouraging Timothy to work at his gift of teaching so that all of the community will see his growth. He must do so through practice and repetition.

ʃ PRACTICAL POINTS

We might not feel like our work is as important as preaching the Gospel. Maybe the product you sell isn't as essential to salvation. But I would caution you not to take what you do so lightly. Yes, sales may not be as important as salvation, but that does not mean it is of no value. Nor does it mean that you should not be the very best in your sales job. Kobe didn't preach the Gospel, but he was the best basketball player of his era. You can be the same in your line of work. The practical points for this chapter are three: constantly learn, repeat the fundamentals and always stay a beginner.

Anyone who wants to succeed in life, in their career especially, must be an eternal student. I once heard a Navy commander at the University of Oklahoma tell his ensigns that "good leaders are voracious readers". That always stuck with me. To be a voracious reader one must constantly devour books. I'm sure many of you are voracious readers. I mean, come on, you're reading this book! But if you're like me, you notice that once you've read a book and some time passes by, you can't quite remember the essential points or message the author wanted to convey. So, read it again. It really is that simple. Read it again. "Repetition taught the donkey." Try as I might, I'm still the donkey. So, I read my books over and over again. My favorite book other than the Bible is *Essentialism*, by Greg McKeown. I've read that book seventeen times and counting. And I cannot tell you how many times I've read the Bible. I want to know it so that I can teach it well. So, I read it and then repeat. If I'm the donkey, then repetition is my great teacher.

Second, don't be afraid to practice the fundamentals of your work over and over again. Once we master the basic tasks of our job, it is easy to leave them behind and move on to bigger challenges. But while you advance, you cannot stop practicing the basic moves that made you successful in the first place. The basic tasks in our career are fundamentals for a reason. They are the foundations upon which the rest of our work is built. If neglected, our proficiency—and therefore our success—will vanish. Remember, Kobe was drafted to the NBA and left the draft to go shoot free throws, the most basic shot in the game of basketball. Never stop practicing the fundamentals.

Lastly, have the mindset of being a novice. Somewhat connected to practicing the fundamentals noted above in practical point number two, maintaining the novice mindset is an excellent way to keep repetition at the forefront of your work ethic. When things are unfamiliar or new to us, we tend to give them extra care and dedicate inordinate amounts of time to mastering them. How did the first meal you ever cooked taste? I bet the second time you prepared it the result was better. Did you master your high school language requirement overnight? Or did you have to spend countless hours the night before your exam flipping through a stack of note cards? What about driving for the first time? Did you fly out of the gates ready to navigate the Indy 500? My fifteen-year old daughter Sophia is learning to drive now, so I know the answer to that question. Even though she is very good, conscientious and safety-first minded, she is definitely not as good a driver as I am. But with all the repetition she's convinced her mother and me to give her, she is way better than the first time she got behind the wheel. I have no doubt she will become a better driver than me someday.

Imagine if we never lost that mindset. What if we looked at life as though we were only at the beginning and dedicated the time and effort to the repetition needed to master new things? We would have a lot less people who think they know everything, and we would instead build an army of explorers who practice and repeat new skills and ideas to make the world a better place. Don't lose that mindset. Consider yourself a novice, find a skill you want to master and spend time practicing it. And then repeat.

Go get some.

30

DON'T YOU EVER QUIT

I don't really watch a lot of television, but a couple of years ago as I was watching a show, two commercials came on back to back that really struck me. The first one was for Weight Watchers. Weight Watchers, as you probably know, is a company that sells a plan with meals to help support their clients to lose weight, become healthier, look good and be attractive to the opposite sex. The commercial that followed it was for a company selling ladies' lingerie, such as bras and underwear. But it wasn't Victoria's Secret. In fact, the models were as far away from Victoria's Secret as you could imagine. They were plus-sized ladies wearing undergarments in the commercial.

The goal of advertisers is to present perceived goals that we should adopt, things that we should aspire to and exceptional behavior that we should commit to. Companies go further and tell us that if we use their product, attaining the goals they've set for us will be easy. This is clear in the message from Weight Watchers. The commercial started by telling us to be exceptional, be beautiful, be attractive to the other sex, be healthy. All that is required is to subscribe to their meal plan and eat their food. But then the very next commercial basically said, "Well, you're never going to make it, so you may as well quit on it and buy plus-size garments." The timing and placement of the two ads was peculiar. One company gave a goal and an easy plan to achieve it, whereas the next company said there was no way of achieving that goal, so one might as well quit.

I'm not saying that all of us need to be like Victoria's Secret models, but I'm saying the first commercial told us to go for exceptional. And then the very next thing we got pounded with was, "Nah, you're going to be mediocre. Just accept it and let us sell you some plus-size garments."

℘ DON'T YOU EVER QUIT IN CONTEXT

We see this type of quitter's mentality all over the place, even in professional sports. I remember an article on *ESPN.com* a few years ago about a storied franchise, the Cleveland Browns. For those who follow the NFL or know anything about football, in 2017 the Cleveland Browns went 0-16. That means they lost sixteen games that season and they didn't win any games. Obviously, every single football team starts the year with one goal, and that's to win the Super Bowl. Not one franchise has a goal to lose all sixteen games.

Naturally, one would assume the Cleveland Browns also started the season with the goal of winning the Super Bowl. But the powerful part about the story is that there was a parade in Cleveland shortly after that season to celebrate what they called "the perfect season." A perfectly miserable season: zero wins, sixteen losses. There were 4,000 Cleveland Browns fans who went to the parade. One of the organizers said on national TV, "Yeah, it [stinks]. We would much rather be preparing for the playoffs, but this is what we got. So, we'll celebrate what we got. We got zero and sixteen, so we'll have a parade."[16] Unbelievable.

Advertising presents us an ideal of what an exceptional person should be. And then, almost in the same breath, it will say, "You're never going to make it. You're going to suffer in mediocrity. You should just quit."

---

[16] https://www.theringer.com/nfl/2018/1/8/16861824/cleveland-browns-perfect-season-parade

❦ GOD'S INPUT

Contrasted to this mediocrity, we find a remarkable story in the first chapter of the Gospel of John. John the Baptist, upon seeing Jesus said, "Behold the lamb of God who takes away the sins of the world," (Jn. 1:29). He takes away the sins of the world! What task is more exceptional than that? What goal is larger than that? What task could God have set before someone that could be greater than taking away the sins of the world? None of us were ever asked to do that. None of us ever will be asked to do that. Only God Himself could take away the sins of the world, and He did so by sending His Son to become a human being like us and, ultimately, to go to the Cross.

Notice that during Jesus' journey to take away the sin of the world, a multitude of challenges were set before Him. Again, no harder task has ever been set before any other human being. There were ample opportunities for Jesus to quit. On His journey people made fun of Him. On one instance they claimed He was possessed by the devil. They spit on Him. They beat Him. Those who loved Him ran away from Him at His darkest hour. They threw Him in jail. They put a fake purple robe on Him. They put a crown of thorns on His head to mock Him as a king. They tortured Him. His kinsmen disavowed Him and even made Him carry the very Cross that they would nail Him upon just a few moments later. And He suffered greatly with agonizing and embarrassing, horrible pain. Finally, He died on that Cross.

It would have been way easier to quit. To think of it logically, if Jesus is indeed the Son of God, could He not have snapped His fingers and called a gazillion angels to come down and crush those who were persecuting Him? He could have escaped the horrible fate of the Cross and lived a pretty swag life. But nowhere in the Gospel, at no point in the entire story, does Jesus ever quit. He never gives up. Of course, He was tempted to quit. In the garden of Gethsemane, knowing the fate that lay ahead of Him, Jesus faced the temptation to quit. He asked God the Father if there was another way, something not as horrible as the Cross. If there was, "let this cup pass." Nevertheless, He did not submit to His own desire to quit. He pushed on to finish what was set before Him (Cf. Mt 26:39).

As odd as it may sound to some, there is great comfort in knowing that the Lord never quit. The entirety of crucifixional living is revealed in the Christ story. Indeed, it *is* the story! In spite of the sufferings He faced, Jesus did not quit, and through His endurance of all that was thrown at Him, even a horrible death, He completed the task He was given. He conquered the greatest of all monsters: Death. Comfort comes not from quitting but in knowing that as great a monster as you and I may have to face, none of them are as big and as scary and as powerful as the monster God the Father set before Jesus Christ. If the Cross can conquer the biggest monster, then it can certainly conquer ours.

In our own lives, we have so many challenges before us and so many things for which we aspire to be exceptional. We want to be great people. We want to be great husbands and great wives. We want to run successful businesses, or if we work in the corporate world, we want to be successful in our positions. If we're students, we want to have great grades.

When thinking about the difficulty of attaining those goals, we find ways to convince ourselves to take an easier and more comfortable road, or worse, to quit. We talk like those commercials noted at the beginning of the chapter that say, "Well, you don't really want to be that thin and beautiful and attractive. You just want to be healthy." No, you don't. You're not fooling me. The desire to be great is in our DNA. Like I said, we're not all going to be as thin as Victoria's Secret models, but the reality of it is that we all want to be exceptional. It's in us. You can say you don't want to be great, but you're fooling no one but yourself.

That's why the health industry is perpetually a thriving business. They do well because we all want the kind of greatness they offer. And yet during the journey, we find that at any moment—really at every moment—it's hard. It becomes a challenge. When the time to fight arises and we don't really want to fight, what do we often end up doing? We end up quitting.

But there's a path that we've been called to follow. A path called the Way of the Warrior Saint. It's an incredible journey of a sacrificial life, a Christ-like life, where we put aside the desire and the temptation to quit. Don't you ever quit. Ever.

℘ PRACTICAL POINTS

To become exceptional people, there are a few final practical steps we should follow. First, I want you to say it out loud: "I will never quit." Let yourself hear yourself say it. There is power in the spoken word. Use your power to motivate yourself in to action. You're the only one you need to convince. Even better, write it down in your Warrior Saints journal. If you don't have one, you better get one. Write it down. It's powerful when you write words. "I will never quit." You have to begin to believe that you won't quit. There will be moments—man, there will be a *lot* of moments—where you're going to be tempted to quit. That's when you go back to that journal and remind yourself, "I will never quit."

Yes, there will be times when you fail at one of your goals. For example, you might say, "Today I am going to eat totally healthy." And then all of a sudden you find that you've eaten a whole bag of Doritos. Okay, you fell down. Get back up. But don't quit. It's not over. If God gives you another breath, get back up. "I will never quit." Say it out loud. And write it down.

Second, think laterally. Conventional wisdom commands us to always be moving forward. I agree that we should always be moving forward toward our goals. But sometimes in that forward movement, we come up against a wall that stops us in our tracks. So naturally, we try to knock it down. When that doesn't work, we try to climb over the wall. When we realize the wall is really tall, we try to dig underneath it. I'm going to dig a trench and I'm going to come up on the other side. In the midst of our digging, we notice that the ground is hard. Frustrated, we continue to push or climb or dig until it's so hard we quit.

What if instead we went around the wall? What if moving forward meant we had to step sideways first? While some call that thinking outside the box, I prefer to call it lateral thinking. What if we came up with a new idea and were unafraid to try something different? What if a lateral move made all the difference? Is your business failing? Are you struggling because you have all these widgets you need to sell and you're not able to sell them? What if instead of washing your hands and blaming it on the economy or your competition you say, "I'm going to try something different, something new, something radical, something simple that no one else has ever thought of before." There's always another way and I bet you can find it if you don't quit.

Third, you have to take massive action. We're Americans and we have everything in the world. We literally have the best of everything in the world. And so, we want everything in the world to be easy and quick. But when it's not easy and quick, what do we do? We quit. Don't you ever quit. Remember that the empty tomb came through the great effort and suffering of the Cross. Likewise, success in your life, being exceptional in your job, in your marriage, in your career, in your relationships, in your health, in school, comes through your own cross. And don't you ever quit.

Somebody may be smarter than you. Somebody may be stronger than you. Somebody may be faster than you. But they will never outwork you if you don't let them. Take massive action while also recognizing that you're going to fail sometimes. In the Roman Catholic tradition, Jesus fell while carrying His Cross. Twice. And He got up. Both times. Don't you ever, ever quit. Take massive action. Don't let anyone ever outwork you.

Remember, as you are facing the challenges that come your way, to be exceptional human beings, to be what God created you to be, you must take massive action. Leave the beaches and the shores of mediocrity and enter into the ocean of excellence. You enter into the ocean of excellence by being a Warrior Saint. Do so with three very simple, practical steps. Say it out loud, think laterally and outwork everyone.

Go get some.

CONCLUSION

I want to conclude by thanking each of you for taking the time to read *The Way of the Warrior Saint*. I'm honored that you took the time to do so. My prayer is that in spite of my limited abilities I was able to offer you some insight to help you become the Warrior Saint God created you to be. The heroes we've visited throughout this book have exhibited what it means to live a crucifixional life. They offer inspiration by showing how a fighting spirit can overcome all of life's obstacles. Their stories prove that monsters can indeed be conquered.

If you take anything away from this text, let it be this: you, too, can become a Warrior Saint and conquer your monsters by living a crucifixional life. Please don't submit to the temptation of believing that you are not as heroic as the characters in this book. Nothing could be further from the truth. Remember, His Son, our Lord and Savior Jesus Christ is "the image of the invisible God, the first-born of all creation," (Col. 1:15). And you were made in His image and after His likeness (Gen. 1:26). St. Paul draws the line perfectly when he says, "For a man ought not to cover his head, since he is the image and glory of God," (1 Cor. 11:7). Do you see? The that same divine spark is inside all of you. God put it there when He created you.

Simply put, that means you are of great value and have been given a high purpose. Your job as a Warrior Saint is to discover your purpose and accomplish it. Along the Way, you will face monsters and the temptation to quit. But I believe in you. You have the power to succeed in whatever you endeavor to do in life. Instead of submitting to fear, face your monsters and crush them by always doing the hard things. Do this by living a life of the Cross: a crucifixional life. And don't you ever quit.

It's time to go get some.

SELECT BIBLIOGRAPHY

All biblical citations are from *The New Oxford Annotated Bible with the Apocrypha, Expanded Edition*, 1962, Revised Standard Version unless otherwise noted.

New International Version. Biblica, 22 March 2020, www.biblica.com/bible/niv.

Blumenthal, Daniel M. and Gold, Mark S. "Neurobiology of food addiction." *National Library of Medicine*. 13 July 2010, pubmed.ncbi.nlm.nih.gov/20495452

Briner, Bob and Pritchard, Ray. *Leadership Lessons of Jesus: Timeless Wisdom for Leaders in Today's World*. New York: Gramercy Books. 1995.

Cardone, Grant. *The 10 X Rule: The Only Difference Between Success and Failure*. Hoboken, NJ: John Wiley and Sons, Inc. 2011.

Clear, James. *Atomic Habits: An Easy and Proven Way to Build Good Habits & Break Bad Ones*. Westminster, London, England: Penguin Classics. 2018.

Collins, Jim. *Good to Great: Why Some Companies Make the Leap and Others Don't*. New York: Harper Collins. 2001.

Durant, W. *The Story of Philosophy: The Lives and Opinions of the World's Greatest Philosophers*. New York: Simon & Schuster, revised edition 1933.

Ellement, John. "Rich Hill acted in 'tumultuous manner' toward Foxborough police, leading to his arrest, report says." *The Boston Globe*, 24 December 2019, www.bostonglobe.com/ 2019/12/24/metro/rich-hill-acted-tumultuous-manner-toward-foxborough-police-leading-his-arrest-report-says.

Gordievsky. "Iverson Practice!" 15 April 2006. *YouTube*, youtu.be/eGDBR2L5kz.

Gunnars, Kris. "10 Similarities Between Sugar, Junk Food and Abusive Drugs." *Healthline*, 23 September 2014, www.healthline.com/nutrition/10-similarities-between-junk-foods-and-drugs.

Harvilla, Rob. "Walk of Shame: A Report from the Cleveland Browns 0-16 Parade." *The Ringer*, 8 January 2018, www.theringer.com/nfl/2018/1/8/16861824/cleveland-browns-perfect-season-parade.

Hilliard, Jena. "Is Alcohol a Depressant?" *Addiction Center,* 24 April 2019, www. addiction center.com/alcohol/is-alcohol-a-depressant/

Keller, Gary and Papasan, Jay. The ONE Thing: *The Surprisingly Simple Truth Behind Extraordinary Results.* Austin, TX: Bard Press. 2014.

Maxwell, John. *The 21 Indispensable Qualities of a Leader: Becoming the Person Others Will Want to Follow.* Nashville, TN: Thomas Nelson, Inc. 1999.

McKeown, Greg. *Essentialism: The Disciplined Pursuit of Less.* New York: Crown Business. 2014.

Moran, Brian P. and Lennington, Michael. *The 12 Week Year: Get More Done in 12 Weeks Than Others Do in 12 Months.* Hoboken, NJ: John Wiley and Sons, Inc. 2013.

Sinek, Simon. *Start with Why: How Great Leaders Inspire Everyone to Take Action.* New York: Penguin Group. 2009.

Sivers, Derek. "Hell Yeah or No: What's Worth Doing." *Derek Sivers.com,* sive.rs/n.

Walia, Harneet, M.D. "Put the Phone Away! 3 Reasons Why Looking at It Before Bed is a Bad Habit." *Cleveland Clinic,* 22 April 2019, health.clevelandclinic. org/put-the-phone-away-3-reasons-why-looking-at-it-before-bed-is-a-bad-habit/#:~:text=closer%20to%20bedtime .-,Dr.,can%20contribute%20to%20 poor%20sleep

Zanetti, Gabriella. "Gamma-aminobutyric acid (GABA): A Molecule of Relaxation." *University of Bristol School of Chemistry,* July 2015, www.chm.bris.ac.uk/motm/ gaba/gabajm.htm.